CULTURE SHOCK!

SUCCEED
IN
BUSINESS

The essential guide for business and investment

India

Hiru Bijlani

TIMES BOOKS INTERNATIONAL
Singapore • Kuala Lumpur

The publishers would like to thank S.S. Panicker, Attaché (Information and Culture), High Commisssion of India, Singapore, for his invaluable contributions to this book.

Photo credits: All photographs by Joginder Chawla

Published by Times Books International
an imprint of Times Editions Pte Ltd
Times Centre
1 New Industrial Road
Singapore 536196
Fax: (65) 285 4871 Tel: (65) 284 8844
e-mail: te@corp.tpl.com.sg

Online Bookstore:
http://www.timesone.com.sg/te

Times Subang
Lot 46, Subang Hi-Tech Industrial Park
Batu Tiga
40000 Shah Alam
Selangor Darul Ehsan
Malaysia
Fax & Tel: (603) 736 3517
E-mail: cchong@tpg.com.my

Printed in Singapore

ISBN 981 204 7328

Contents

Acknowledgements

Thanks to Jeevan and Tanya for helping to type, compile and proofread the first draft. Thanks also to Suresh Surana and Associates for their assistance in providing some material for the book.

This book is dedicated to the people of India whose
economic destiny has arrived.

Introduction

The Indian subcontinent covers a total land area of 3.3 million square kilometres. The seventh largest and second most populous country in the world, it is bordered by the Indian Ocean, the Arabian Sea and the Bay of Bengal. India's neighbours are Pakistan, China, Nepal, Bhutan, Myanmar (previously called Burma), Bangladesh and Sri Lanka. A democratic republic of 930 million people, India is made up of 25 states and seven union territories. The capital is New Delhi.

From independence in 1947 until early 1991, India's economy was based on a socialist model. In other words, the state had considerable control over the economy. This brought about rapid industrial development in certain major industries like steel and engineering. With state control, however, came bureaucratic inefficiency and huge losses incurred by the Exchequer. When the country descended into an economic abyss in early 1991 as a result of its corrupt, inefficient and socialist model of economic development, the government launched a reform programme, focusing on large-scale foreign investments. Foreign investors flocked to the country.

The policy of economic liberalisation, initiated by P.V. Narasimha Rao, Manmohan Singh, Montek Singh Ahluwalia and P. Chidambaram, has brought about remarkable changes to the Indian economy. India's gross domestic product (GDP) had grown only by 2% to 4 % per annum during most of the post-independence period. Its per capita income of US$300 was one of the lowest in the world. In the post-liberalisation period, however, economic development has accelerated. India's economy is expected to sustain growth rates of 5 to 7 %, making it the world's fourth largest economy by the year 2020.

Some regions of the country and some sections of the Indian society have made dramatic economic progress. India's middle class, for instance, is substantial and expanding rapidly. However, a large proportion of the population continue to live in abject poverty. Problems, such as corruption, population control, economic disparity, illiteracy, a huge and expensive bureaucracy and poor infrastructure, are the greatest challenges facing India. This is set against the backdrop of the country's ever volatile relationship with Pakistan, which some see as a constant threat to its economic progress.

A sound knowledge of history is essential to business success in any part of the world. This is especially true of India, for history pervades many aspects of life for the Indians. By giving readers a comprehensive historical account of India—a civilisation that dates back some 5,000 years—this book sets up the framework for understanding the workings and the contemporary business environment of the country. In addition, it highlights matters of crucial importance to an investor, such as the evolution of the new economic policy of 1991. An indispensable guide to the Indian stock markets, the book further describes opportunities for investment presented by the country and various aspects of joint ventures, including the selection of suitable joint venture partners.

Lucid discussion of the historical background and contemporary practices will help the reader gain an insight into the Indian psyche of doing business as well as capitalise on an economy that is showing great promise. Indeed many see India as a "caged tiger waiting to be unleashed", impacting the world's economy by providing challenges and opportunities for investment. Understanding India is the key to transforming an enigma into a fortune.

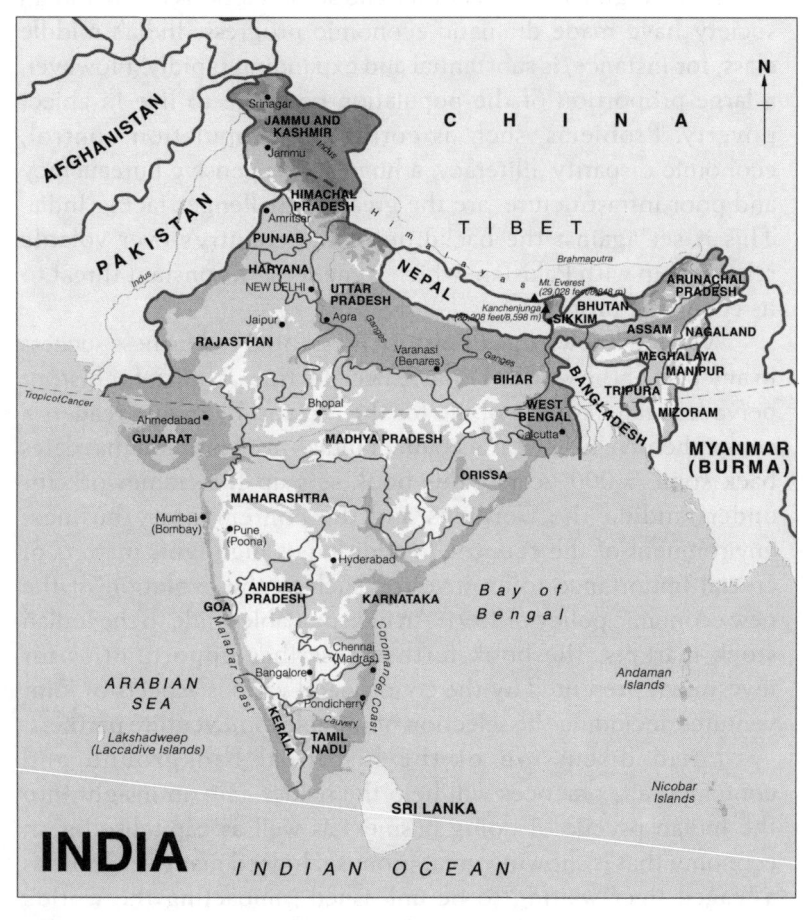

Map of India

CHAPTER 1

Indian History for the Business Person

A sound knowledge of Indian history and culture will help a foreign business person understand his/her Indian colleagues better and stand him/her in good stead for business success in India. Once the foreign business person grasps the intricate cultural context in which meetings and negotiations take place, he/she will have a definite advantage over those who do not.

History: A Snapshot

India's history goes back more than 5,000 years. A clear record of Indian civilization dates back to the Indus Valley Civilization (3500 B.C.)—a growth of villages and towns that eventually developed a distinct culture.

In 1924, archaeologists discovered two ancient cities. They were Mohenjo-Daro and Harappa in what is Pakistan today. They also found remnants of many other smaller towns, from Gujarat on the western coast of India to the Himalayas in the north. Scholars believe that a sea trade existed between north western India and the Persian Gulf from 2000 B.C.

For much of its later history, India was split into small states ruled by warring kings and princes. Powerful empires rose and fell, uniting the smaller states for varying lengths of time. The last of these empires—the British Empire—ended its rule on 15 August 1947. Three years later, India became a democratic republic.

The history of early India is known mainly from religious texts or the four *Vedas*: the *Rig Veda*, the *Sama Veda*, the *Yajur Veda* and the *Artharva Veda*. The Vedas form the basis of Hindu religion and philosophy. They were transmitted orally by generations of priests before being written down. The Vedic and other mythological literature reveal that the Aryans, who came to India around 1500 B.C., were organised into tribes, thus suggesting they came from Central Europe and Asia.

Hinduism

Hinduism, the religion of more than 85% of Indians, has no founder or prophet and reincarnation is its basic tenet. Hindus believe their present position in life is on account of their karma or actions in past lives. In other words, people live their lives in accordance with a predetermined destiny. Life is a cycle of births and rebirths. Death is not an end but a transfer of the soul from one body to another. The ultimate quest is for *moksha* or liberation from the life cycle by living a pure and perfect life.

Hinduism permeates every aspect of life for most Hindu Indians. The vast pantheon of Hindu deities is manifest everywhere, from commonplace daily chores to work, education and politics. In offices across India, it is quite common to see prayers offered to a Hindu deity. If you are setting up a new project, plant or machinery, your Indian counterpart will most likely pick an auspicious date based on astrological advice.

Besides the Hindus, Muslims are the most prominent religious group in India. Christians, Sikhs, Jains and Buddhists too have a strong religious presence in India.

Popular Deities

The *Puranas* are mythological stories that focus on the Vedic gods and their heroic actions. They comprise two great epics: the *Mahabharata* and the *Ramayana*. In Hinduism, the god Brahma is the creator, the god Vishnu is the preserver and the god Shiva is the destroyer. The three are often depicted in a trinity. Other gods and goddesses, who come alive in mythological epics, are depicted in human or semi-human form and are also worshipped.

Society

The stratification of Hindu society is based on the four hierarchical classes: Brahmins (priests and teachers), Kshatriyas (rulers and warriors), Vaishyas (merchants and cultivators) and Shudras (labourers and servants). Each class is assigned specific religious and social duties. The first class is given full access to religious texts and rituals. Unfortunately, as the last group's duties involve contact with dirt and death, they are classified as untouchables. In India today, although remnants of the caste system still exist in some states, discrimination against untouchables is a criminal offence, a result of the untiring efforts of Mahatma Gandhi and others.

Spread of literacy, urbanisation, constitutional guarantees against discrimination based on caste, empowerment of backward castes through various measures, vigilant institutions of democracy (parliament, press, an independent judiciary, etc.) have vastly changed society's social structure. In fact, reservation of seats in legislatures and government service has resulted in a large number of backward classes and castes holding positions of authority.

In ancient India, social status was further subcategorised by family and occupation. For example, a Vaishya would usually end up being a jewellery seller, cloth merchant or farmer. A person's *jati* determined his or her caste and laid down restrictions on all aspects of life, including food consumption, religious obligations, contact with other people of other castes and choice of marriage partners. Marrying someone of a different caste often resulted in ostracism from both family and community, leaving the couple stranded in a society where caste affiliation was important. This system of categorising people is still adhered to by some sections of the society.

You Do Your Work; I Do Mine

A couple of middle managers of a company meet with a foreign expert in his office to discuss the installation of a new machine. It is agreed that the machine be placed next to the facsimile machine. However, a desk has to be moved so the machine can be hooked up. The managers leave. A few hours later, the desk has still not been moved. When asked, one of the managers explains to the foreign expert that the person who does such things—the peon or office boy—has not yet arrived. The peon then arrives. The managers stand aside while the peon struggles to carry the desk through the door.

The foreigner working in India may experience this kind of outright resistance one group shows for the work of the other. It comes about as a result of adhering strictly to the division of labour from birth. In most offices today (except government offices), the peon has been dispensed with. The executive is required to do everything, and this includes making his or her own coffee.

Persian and Greek Invasions

In its early history, India's fine cities and prosperous villages attracted the attention of foreign invaders. In 530 B.C., the Persian Emperor Cyrus the Great subjugated many tribes in the Hindu Kush Mountains. The Persians seized the province of Gandhara and parts of the Punjab. Two hundred years later, an even more formidable conqueror, Alexander the Great of Macedonia, invaded India. Alexander defeated and overran the mighty Persian Empire. He also founded a number of kingdoms in Asia. His invasion of India in 326 B.C. was the first recorded military encounter between the people of ancient India and the Greeks.

The Rise and Fall of the Mauryas

In 325 B.C., Chandragupta became the first king of the Mauryan Empire, and after Alexander's death, he drove away the Greek garrison and took control of the Greek settlements. His rule extended from the north to the far south.

The Mauryan Empire reached the height of its rule when King Ashoka ascended the throne in 269 B.C. The empire began to decline after Ashoka's reign. At around 180 B.C., the Brahmanic dynasty of the Shungas replaced the Mauryan Empire. Repeated invasions of northern India by the Greeks, the Parthians of Persia and the various Turkish tribes of Central Asia led to constant wars and political instability in the country.

In A.D. 100, another Central Asian tribe called the Kushanas invaded India. They established a powerful empire under the Kushan ruler, Kanishka. This empire extended from Sinkiang in China to Varanasi in eastern India. The vastness of the Kushan Empire and its political success were matched by its cultural achievements. In both art and religion, the Kushan rulers were influenced by Indian, Greek and Persian traditions.

Sanskrit, Philosophy and the Arts

Sanskrit culture was greatly influenced by Western thought and civilization. This was a result of contact with the Greeks, Romans and Persians. Varahamihira, an Indian philosopher, wrote that the Greeks, although "impure" (all foreigners were considered somewhat unclean due to their personal hygiene habits) according to Vedic ritualistic practices, should be honoured because they excelled in science, mathematics and the arts.

In the fifth century B.C., Panini (a linguist) wrote down the rules of Sanskrit grammar in standard form. In the second century B.C., Patanjali supplemented Panini's work and laid down all the major rules regarding the science of language and sounds produced by the human voice. Indian mathematicians began to use the number zero and negative numbers. Art, literature and philosophy flourished during this period.

Trade with the West

Western influence seeped into India not only from the Greek, Persian and Central Asian invasions, but also from the land and sea trade that connected the Indian subcontinent, the Middle East and the Roman Empire. In A.D. 100, Pliny, a Roman historian, maintained that each year a vast quantity of gold and silver left the Roman Empire to pay for the spices, textiles and other luxury goods imported from India. Details of this seaborne trade were described by an unknown sailor or merchant of Alexandria, a port town in Egypt, in a book called the *Periplus of the Erythraean Sea*.

Exported goods included spices, cotton and silk cloth, perfumes, aromatic gums, rare wood and various types of grains. Archaeologists excavating sites in western and southern India have found a large quantity of Roman coins, pottery, glass and other objects at sites that once served as important trading ports on the Indian coast. The author of *Periplus of the Erythraean Sea* also refers to the Greek discovery of the annual monsoon winds, which made it possible for ships to sail to India from the Red Sea or the Persian Gulf and return home within one calendar year. A sailor called Hippalos was said to have made the first trading voyage to India.

The Gupta Empire, the Hunas and Harsha Vardhana

The rise of the Gupta dynasty in A.D. 300 brought about a peaceful era that lasted until A.D. 500. Each Gupta ruler expanded the empire. Between A.D. 470 and 520, China, India and the Roman world faced a new threat from the Hunas of Central Asia. They were descendants of Turkish-speaking warriors and were invincible in battle. After founding major kingdoms in Hungary, the Hunas moved into India. The last Gupta ruler to hold out against the Hunas was Skandagupta.

Huan Tsang, a Chinese pilgrim who travelled across India for 14 years from A.D. 630–644, vividly describes the great Harsha Vardhana, who ruled northern India from A.D. 606 to 647. Chinese rulers sent three special missions to Harsha's court during this period.

The Coming of Islam

Islam spread when the Arabs moved from Arabia to the Mediterranean and the Iranian highland. In A.D. 712, Muslims from Arabia sent an overland military expedition to Sindh, an important trading centre. The expedition was significant because it succeeded in founding an Islamic kingdom in parts of India.

The Arab caliphs made no serious effort to push the frontiers of Islam into the Indian subcontinent despite the growth of commercial and cultural ties between the Islamic Middle East and India. Many Muslim merchants, who conducted trade at the ports of Gujarat and the Malabar Coast, settled in the cities. Eventually, their families formed sizeable colonies. The local rulers allowed the Muslims to build mosques and practise their religion.

In A.D. 800, Jahizan, an Arab writer from Baghdad, gave an extraordinary account of Indian intellectual achievements. The Indians, he wrote, led the world in science and mathematics. They possessed a script capable of expressing the sounds of all the languages and many numerals, had many long treatises, as well as a deep understanding of philosophy.

Turkish Raids

Between A.D. 1000 and 1030, Mahmud of Ghazni led a series of devastating raids into India. He was a soldier of remarkable ability and inspired his followers with a zeal for conquest and the lure of financial rewards. The loot from India made Sultan Mahmud and the Ghaznavi Kingdom in Afghanistan rich. It also boosted the economy in the Middle East.

The Delhi Sultanate

In 1192, Muhammad of Ghor invaded the Punjab. He defeated the Rajput chief, Prithvi Raj Chauhan, at the second battle of Tarain. Within 10 years, his general conquered most of northern India. Muhammad appointed a Turkish slave leader, Qutbud Din Aybak, to consolidate the Muslim conquest of India.

The Rajput rulers of northern India were unable to offer any real resistance to the Delhi sultans. This was partly because they were disunited and partly because the military tactics of the Turks—based on cavalry—were new to them. Indian rulers still relied on infantry with war elephants.

In 1294, the Muslim rulers of Delhi began to expand into the south of India. The military expeditions brought large financial rewards to the Delhi Sultanate, such as tributes paid by the Hindu princes and treasures looted from the rich cities.

In 1258, the Mongols conquered Baghdad and parts of the Middle East, and began to move towards India. The rulers of Delhi needed money to pay for a large army to meet this challenge, so the richest coastal provinces in Gujarat were brought under the permanent control of Delhi.

Increased financial resources from the southern Indian campaigns and a better taxation system enabled the Delhi Sultanate to resist the attempts of the invaders. However, in 1398, the ferocious Mongol conqueror, Tamerlane, attacked Delhi, and the Muslim Empire in India disintegrated into a number of warring kingdoms. In 1350, the Hindu state of Vijaynagar was founded on the Deccan Plateau. This brought the whole of southern India under Hindu control and served as a barrier to Muslim advance.

During the next 200 years, the conquests of the Mongols, who came to be known as the Mughals, created one of the best administered empires that India had ever known. The first Mughal conqueror was Babar, a descendant of Tamerlane. Babar died in 1530 and was succeeded by his son Humayun, who in turn was succeeded by Akbar, perhaps the best remembered and most benevolent of the Mughal rulers.

Akbar the Great and the Mughal Government

Akbar enjoyed the company of scholars and artists and built vast monuments, palaces and entire cities. He built a new capital at Fatehpur Sikri in Agra to mark the conquest of Gujarat and the birth of his first son, Salim. The new capital was abandoned about 10 years later. It is known for its impressive collection of Islamic and Hindu architecture. Akbar's conquests subdued the powerful Rajput princes, especially after his army captured the fortress of Chitor in 1567.

One of Akbar's greatest achievements was the introduction of a system of land taxation, which was administrated by his Hindu minister, Raja Todar Mal. Akbar, together with his finance ministers, reorganised the land taxation system and linked it to the administration of the empire.

He also started a new administrative system known as *jagirdari*. Instead of being paid a salary from the central treasury, a civil officer in charge of a district was given a specific plot of land for a limited period. He was aided by a military officer who was expected to keep a certain number of cavalry soldiers and pay them out of his *jagir* or land grant. These units of cavalry comprised the Mughal standing army. The holders of the jagir were moved from place to place every two to three years to prevent them from eventually becoming landowners.

Akbar's officials divided the empire into provinces and districts. A military officer, often a prince of the royal house, acted as the viceroy of the provinces. A separate official called the *dewan* collected taxes and sent the money to the central treasury at Delhi. The reforms resulted in economic prosperity for the Mughals.

Akbar was succeeded by Jahangir (1605–1627), Shah Jahan (1628–1658) and Aurangzeb (1658–1707). Shah Jahan was a great supporter of the arts, especially architecture. In Agra, he built the famous Taj Mahal as a monument of love for his dead queen. His last years, however, were troubled by a rebellion organised by his son, Aurangzeb, who later deposed Shah Jahan to seize the throne for himself. Shah Jahan eventually died a prisoner in the fortress of Agra.

Aurangzeb imposed a poll tax on non-Muslims during his reign. After his death in 1707, the Mughal Empire went into decline. The final blow to the Mughal Empire came in 1739 when the Persian conqueror Nadir Shah invaded India. Nadir Shah fled to Persia with the loot from Delhi and the government treasury. The treasures included the Peacock Throne, which was used by the later rulers of Iran, and the kohinoor, one of the biggest diamonds in the world. The diamond is now part of the British crown jewels.

Europeans in India

In 1497, the Portuguese king, Manuel I, sent the navigator Vasco da Gama to find a sea route to India via the Cape of Good Hope at the southern tip of Africa. Da Gama reached the port of Calicut on the Malabar Coast on 18 June 1498 and his fleet returned to Lisbon, Portugal in 1499. The Portuguese set up a trading empire in the Indian Ocean, controlling the major sea routes between India, the Middle East and Southeast Asia. They made Goa their capital in India. Portuguese supremacy in the Indian Ocean lasted for over a hundred years.

The British East India Company was founded in 1600. The Dutch East India Company was formally incorporated two years later. The arrival of the British and Dutch in India, however, threatened the Portuguese who tried to monopolise the Asian trade.

Portuguese hostility and the long-drawn-out war between the Netherlands and Portugal's neighbour, Spain, made the Dutch East India Company keen to drive the Portuguese out of the spice trade.

The Dutch were much stronger at sea than the Portuguese and within 50 years, they reduced the Portuguese maritime empire in India to a shadow of its past.

The British East India Company, by contrast, was much weaker as it initially did not engage in wars of expansion. In the 1600s, it acquired three independent sovereign settlements in India—Chennai, Mumbai and Calcutta. Each of the settlements grew into a trading port. The ports were fortified with sea walls and cannons. After 1700, the British East India Company was strong enough to equip a large number of ships with arms for trade in the Indian Ocean.

In the 1720s, the French government granted a charter to a French East India Company to trade with India. The French made their headquarters at Pondicherry in southern India. Within 20 years, the French became powerful in India and competed successfully with the British for a slice of the Indian trade. In the 1740s, the French and the British supported rival Indian rulers to further their own cause.

The British Empire

Historians regard the year 1757 as the starting point of the British Empire in India. It took nearly another hundred years for the East India Company and the British government to extend their rule across India. Lord Cornwallis, the governor-general of India, was given the task of reforming the administration in India and establishing good relations with the Indian princes. He set up an independent judicial system that prevented the company's officials from conducting private trade and getting government contracts. He also reformed the police force and the criminal justice system.

Cornwallis's greatest achievement in India was the reorganisation of the land taxation. Previously, agricultural land in Bengal was cultivated by a large number of small farmers who paid rent to a group of *zamindars* or landlords who, in turn, paid taxes to the government. The East India Company, however, tried to collect land taxes directly from company officials or revenue farmers.

Defeat of Tipu Sultan
Cornwallis waged a brief but successful war against Tipu Sultan, the ruler of the Deccan in southern India. With the arrival of Lord Wellesley as governor-general in 1797, British military expansion in India took a new direction. The new governor-general was an outstanding political leader. He was assisted by his brother, General Arthur Wellesley, the future Lord Wellington and victor at the Battle of Waterloo in 1815.

Wellesley regarded Tipu Sultan as a dangerous enemy on the grounds that Tipu had befriended a party of stranded Frenchmen. Wellesley attacked Mysore, and Tipu was killed at the battle of Seringapatam in 1799. The British annexed half of his territory, and the rest was returned to the previous Hindu dynasty, which had been dispossessed of the territory by Tipu's father, Hyder Ali.

Wellesley also waged two wars against the Marathas in the north and the west. By 1804, the military campaigns extended British political power as far as Delhi. The British defeated the Marathas and annexed their territory in 1818. The Sikh state of the Punjab remained independent until the war of 1848 when it came under direct British rule.

British Rule: Government and Trade
The political unity created by the British in India was welcomed by many enlightened Indians. So too were the moves towards social reforms and European-style education. In 1814, the East India Company's charter was renewed for another 30 years. However, the company was no longer permitted to monopolise Indian trade. Trade was now open to British merchants who wished to export

goods manufactured in Britain. The company continued to trade in Indian products until 1833, when all commercial activities were stopped by the British Parliament.

From 1800 to 1830, the economic policy of the East India Company firmly linked Indian financial affairs to the wider economic interests of Britain. The Industrial Revolution of the eighteenth and nineteenth century in Britain created many new opportunities for British businesses to increase their trade with India.

For many years, Indian cotton spinners and weavers supplied finished cloths to markets in Asia, Africa, Europe and the United States. It was, however, difficult for foreigners to compete with the Indian workers. Indians produced goods inexpensively and the technology of spinning and weaving cotton by traditional craft methods was difficult for competitors to master. Once British factory owners learnt the techniques of machine spinning and weaving, they imported cheap raw cotton from the American plantations. Finished cloths from British mills became much cheaper than Indian handloom products. Cotton mills in Lancashire, England, exported more and more cloths to India and by the mid-1800s, much of India's basic needs in cotton clothing were met by British factories. Indian spinners and weavers lost their jobs and had to turn to agriculture to eke out a living.

The East India Company continued selling Indian products in Europe. It also exported opium from India to China in exchange for tea. Historians today agree that land taxes were severe and caused many difficulties for the Indian farmers. Also, the industrial changes did not make the Indian craftworker any better off. Despite these difficulties, the British administration in India did not face any real threat until the revolt of 1857. The revolt started with a mutiny by the Indian army at Meerut.

The horrors of the 1857 mutiny in which the Indian soldiers revolted on the use of cow and pig fat for greasing their cartridges, and the war that followed were lessened to some degree by the lenient and conciliatory policy adopted by Lord Canning, the first governor-general in India to represent the British government directly.

Formal British Takeover of India

In 1876, Queen Victoria became the Empress of India. The title of governor-general was changed to viceroy. The executive council was to assist the viceroy in his duties. Council members became ministers responsible for various state departments. The British viceroy enjoyed great personal power and prestige. He had a large residence and staff, and was free from any control by the people of India. The British government felt that the viceroy should display a degree of pomp and ceremony in order to show the Indians that he was following the same courtly traditions as the great Mughals.

Economics: The Essence of British Rule

Economic issues dominated public debate during the second half of the 1800s. A better transportation network was deemed necessary to transport raw materials from different parts of India to Britain. British engineers, who were good at building railways, constructed a series of major railways in India. By 1870, Calcutta, Delhi, Mumbai and Chennai were connected by railways.

Railway building in India was done for both military and economic reasons. The experience of the 1857 revolt had taught the British army the usefulness of quick transportation, so rail lines were extended to the north-west frontier province. Any threat of invasion by Afghanistan or Russia could now be quickly averted — troops could be sent into the Punjab immediately. The railways also made it possible to transport agricultural produce, such as raw cotton, wheat, oil seeds and indigo, to the ports for export at a much faster rate.

In the 1860s, the American Civil War cut off the supply of American raw cotton to the Lancashire cotton mills. India was expected to make up the shortfall. Cotton cultivation greatly expanded in western India as a result and brought in much cash to cotton farmers. Between 1850 and 1880, the Indian subcontinent suffered a series of harvest failures, but an improved transportation network made it possible to send grains quickly from areas where there was a surplus to areas that experienced food shortages.

Things were going so well for the British in India and elsewhere that it was generally believed that the "sun would never set on the British Empire". However, World War I shattered this belief. The costly war weakened Britain considerably.

Freedom Movement

The Indian nationalist movement started in the early 1880s. At first it was a moderate constitutional movement. A.O. Hume, a liberal Englishman, and a number of liberal-minded westernized Indians founded the Indian National Congress (INC) in 1885.

In its early days, the INC confined itself to an annual debate of political issues. It requested the government to look into the complaints of the people but had no constitutional role. However, some members of the INC were also members of the legislative assembly, which advised the viceroy and the executive committee on the drafting of new laws. In the 1890s, due to the influence of Bal Gangadhar Tilak, a radical thinker and politician, the Indian independence movement gained momentum.

Many Indian soldiers, who fought for Britain during the war and had distinguished themselves on the battlefields of the European and Middle Eastern campaigns, were aware of the process by which political affairs were conducted in Europe. When they returned home, they began demanding political changes through public meetings. The government banned such political meetings.

On 13 April 1919, British Commander General Dyer led Gurkha troops to an illegal meeting in Amritsar in the Punjab. The entrance to the meeting place, the Jallian walla Bagh Garden, was blocked by troops. General Dyer ordered the soldiers to open fire on the crowd. Nearly 400 civilians were killed and another 1,200 wounded. This event soon came to be called the Jallian walla Bagh massacre. It laid the foundation for the freedom movement.

Mahatma Gandhi

Gandhi was born in 1869 in Gujarat. He was trained as a lawyer in England and returned to India for a short period. He then sailed to South Africa to be a lawyer in an Indian firm. There he saw the evils of oppression. One turning point in his life occurred when he was physically thrown out of a "Whites Compartment" in a local train. To protest against racism, he organised the *Satyagraha* movement, a non-violent protest. Later, Gandhi returned to India and joined the INC.

Gandhi's political tactics, which appeared strange to both Europeans and English-educated Indians, appealed to the ordinary people. It was based on the idea of non-violent disobedience through peaceful mass demonstrations (against British rule). He also organised a boycott of British goods in India. Between 1920 and 1921, he launched the Satyagraha Campaign. This turned the independence movement into a popular campaign, but the demonstrations were marred by violent clashes between the police and demonstrators. Gandhi was joined in his efforts by another young Indian politician, Jawaharlal Nehru, who was also educated in England.

New Constitution

In 1935 the British parliament passed the Government of India Act. The act created a new constitution and got Indian politicians into a law-making assembly. The act also led to the creation of

Indian-controlled governments in the provinces. The central government remained under the control of the viceroy and the executive council.

World War II

The outbreak of World War II in 1939 interrupted India's progress towards self-government. The British promised India independence after the war, but members of the INC demanded immediate self-government and refused to contribute to the war effort. After Germany's conquest of France in 1940, India showed more willingness to help Britain and joined in the war effort. Indian troops fought with great courage and skill in various desert campaigns. In 1941, Japan entered the war on the side of Germany. The next year, Japanese troops captured Burma, India's neighbour to the east.

The Allies then built air bases in India and flew supplies to the Chinese to help them fight the Japanese. By the end of 1943, India was a huge supply base and training centre for Allied armies and air forces. During the war, Britain tried to reach an agreement with Indian leaders on the subject of independence. In 1942, it proposed that India be an independent dominion in the British Commonwealth of Nations. The plan was unanimously rejected by all Indian political groups.

In the same year, Gandhi launched another civil disobedience campaign. The entire Congress leadership was arrested, and the leaders were not released until the end of the war. When negotiations began again between the British and the nationalists, they were complicated by a demand from the Muslim League for a separate independent Muslim state in India.

The Muslim League feared that Hindus would dominate independent India. The pertinent unanswered question was whether Muslims would have a separate Islamic state within India or an entirely independent country. The INC or the Congress Party, however, opposed the division of the country into Hindu and Muslim states. The Muslim League leader, Muhammad Ali Jinnah, insisted that Muslims could not live safely in a Hindu-dominated India. The viceroy of India, Viscount Wavell, met with representatives of the various Indian groups to come to a decision.

Jawaharlal Nehru realised that there was no way out of the Hindu-Muslim deadlock. Indian and British leaders then agreed to partition India into separate states. The western part of the Punjab and East Bengal became the independent state of Pakistan on 14 August 1947.

Independence and Partition

India became independent on 15 August 1947. The country's first prime minister was Jawaharlal Nehru. Celebrations marking independence, however, were marred by tragedy. Widespread violence and riots broke out in the two countries, and more than 20 million Hindus and Muslims fled their homes. Many people were attacked and murdered. The leaders of the new nations of India and Pakistan were left with the difficult task of rebuilding their shattered economies.

CHAPTER 2

Understanding the New Republic

India, a union of states, is "a sovereign socialist secular democratic republic" with a parliamentary system of government. The republic is governed in terms of the constitution.

The Constitution

On 26 November 1948, a constituent assembly headed by Dr. B.R. Ambedkar adopted a new constitution for independent India. The constitution came into effect on 26 January 1950.

The national or official language is Hindi, while India's colonial heritage makes English the second official language. Other main languages are Bengali, Telugu, Marathi, Tamil, Urdu, Gujarathi, Malayalam, Kannada, Oriya, Punjabi and Assamese.

The Indian flag is derived from the flag of the Indian National Congress (INC), the party of Mahatma Gandhi and Jawaharlal Nehru. It, therefore, bears much similarity to the party flag. It is a horizontal tricolour of deep saffron, white, and dark green. In the centre of the white band is an emblem taken from a pillar built by Emperor Ashoka (269–232 B.C.). The Sanskrit words below the emblem read as follows: "Truth alone triumphs".

The States and Union Territories

India consists of 25 states and six centrally administered areas called union territories. The states are Andhra Pradesh, Arunachal Pradesh, Assam, Bihar, Goa, Gujarat, Haryana, Himachal Pradesh, Jammu and Kashmir, Karnataka, Kerala, Madhya Pradesh, Maharashtra, Manipur, Meghalaya, Mizoram, Nagaland, Orissa, Punjab, Rajasthan, Sikkim, Tamil Nadu, Tripura, Uttar Pradesh and West Bengal. The union territories are the Andaman and Nicobar Islands, Chandigarh, Dadra and Nagar Haveli, Daman and Diu, Lakshadweep and Pondicherry. The capital, New Delhi, is the seat of the union government and the president, prime minister, and almost all arms of the administration.

Citizenship

The Constitution of India provides for a single citizenship that is uniform across India. Each person born and domiciled in the territory of India is a citizen of the country. Each person whose parent was born in the territory of India for not less than five years immediately preceding the constitution is also considered a citizen of the country. The Citizenship Act of 1955 provides for the acquisition and termination of citizenship.

Fundamental Rights

The constitution offers all citizens some basic freedoms. These are guaranteed in the constitution in the form of six broad categories of Fundamental Rights. They are as follows:

- Right to equality, including equality before the law, prohibition of discrimination on the grounds of religion, race, caste, sex or place of birth and equality of opportunity in matters of employment.
- Right to freedom of speech and expression, assembly association, union, movement, residence and the right to practise any profession or occupation.
- Right against exploitation, prohibiting all forms of forced labour, child labour and traffic in human beings.
- Right to freedom of conscience and freedom for the practice and propagation of religion.
- Right of any section of citizens to conserve their culture, language or script and the right of minorities to establish and administer educational institutions of their choice.
- Right to constitutional remedies for the enforcement of Fundamental Rights.

Fundamental Duties

In the 42nd amendment of the constitution, which was adopted in 1976, Fundamental Duties of Indian citizens were enumerated. Article 51A in part IVA of the constitution deals with these duties. They are as follows:

- To abide by the constitution
- To cherish and follow noble ideals inspired by India's national struggle for freedom
- To defend the country and render national service when called upon to do so
- To promote harmony and instil the spirit of common brotherhood in the people of India that transcend religious, linguistic and regional or sectional diversities

Directive Principles of State Policy

The constitution lays down certain Directive Principles of state policy that are fundamental to governing the country, and it is the duty of the state to apply these principles when making laws.

The principles state that India shall strive to promote the welfare of its people by securing and protecting as effectively as it may a social order in which justice—social, economic and political—prevails in all institutions of the country.

The state shall direct its policy in such a manner as to secure the rights of all men and women to an adequate means of livelihood, equal pay for equal work and within limits of its economic capacity and development, to make effective provisions for securing the right to work, education and to public assistance in the event of unemployment, old age, sickness and disablement or other cases of undeserved want. Some of the important directives relate to provisions for the promotion of international peace and security, just and honourable relations between nations, respect for international law, treaty obligations and settlement of international disputes by arbitration.

Government

India's parliamentary system is modelled on the British one. Parliament consists of the Rajya Sabha (upper house), which is the Council of States, and the Lok Sabha (lower house), which is the House of the People. Important functionaries in the Indian government are the chief election commissioner, the controller and auditor general, and the attorney general.

At the state level, the highest functionaries of the government are the governor who takes on the role of president and the chief minister who takes on the role of prime minister in the central government. There is also a district administration, where the district collector, a civil servant, has the highest level of authority. He/She combines the role of the governor and the chief minister at the state level. The Civil Services is another pillar of the government system and comprises the All India Services, the Central Services and the State Services, from which selected candidates are appointed as bureaucrats to the central and state governments.

The Union Executive

The Union Executive consists of the president, vice-president and a Council of Ministers, with the prime minister as head to aid and advise the president.

President

The president is elected by members of an electoral college, which consists of elected members of the Rajya Sabha, the Lok Sabha and the legislative assemblies of the states in accordance with the system of proportional representation by means of single transferable vote. To secure uniformity among states and the central government, suitable weighting is given to each vote.

The president must be a citizen of India, not less than 35 years of age and must be qualified for election as member of the Lok Sabha. His/Her term of office is five years and he/she is eligible for re-election. His/Her removal from office is in accordance with the procedures prescribed in the constitution. He/She may, by writing to the vice-president, resign from the post.

The executive power of the union is vested in the president and is exercised by him/her either directly or through officers subordinate to him/her. The president summons, addresses and sends messages to parliament; dissolves the Lok Sabha (lower house) when necessary; promulgates ordinances; makes recommendations for introducing financial bills; gives assent to bills; and grants, pardons, reprieves and remits punishment or suspends, remits and commutes sentences.

In the event constitutional machinery fails in a state, the president can assume all or any of the functions of the government of that state. He/She can proclaim a period of emergency in the country if adequately satisfied that the situation warrants it, such as when the security of India or any part of its territory is threatened.

Vice-president

The vice-president is elected by members of an electoral college, which consists of members of the Rajya Sabha and the Lok Sabha in accordance with the system of proportional representation. He/She must be a citizen of India, not less than 35 years of age and eligible for election as member of the Rajya Sabha.

The vice-president's term of office is five years and he/she is eligible for re-election. His/Her removal from office is in accordance with the procedures prescribed in the constitution. The vice-president is the ex-officio chairman of the Rajya Sabha and takes on the role of president when the latter is unable to discharge his/her functions due to absence, illness or any other cause or until the election of a new president (to be held within six months). He/She, while acting as president, ceases to be the chairman of the Rajya Sabha.

Council of Ministers

The Council of Ministers, headed by the prime minister, aids and advises the president in his/her functions. The prime minister is appointed by the president, who in turn appoints other ministers on the advice of the prime minister. The council is collectively responsible to the Lok Sabha.

Rajya Sabha

The constitution states that the Rajya Sabha may consist of 250 members. Out of this figure, 12 are nominated by the president from among those with specialist knowledge or practical experience in such fields as literature, science, arts and social service. There may not be more than 238 representatives from the states and union territories. Rajya Sabha members are elected by elected members of the legislative assemblies of the states in accordance with the system of proportional representation. The Rajya Sabha is not subject to dissolution. One-third of its members retire on expiry of their tenure every second year.

Lok Sabha

The Lok Sabha consists of representatives chosen by direct election on the basis of universal adult suffrage. The maximum strength of the house, as envisaged by the constitution, is now 552. Out of this figure, 530 members represent the states, 20 represent the union territories and not more than two members represent the Anglo-Indian community if the president is of the opinion that the community is not adequately represented in the houses. The total elective membership of the Lok Sabha is distributed among states in such a way that the ratio between the number allotted to each state and the population of that state is uniform for all the states.

The allocation of seats in the present Lok Sabha is based on the 1971 census and the 42nd amendment of the constitution (1976), and will continue to be based on them until the figures of the first census taken after the year 2000 become available. The term of the Lok Sabha, unless dissolved, is five years from the date fixed for its first meeting. However, while a proclamation of emergency is in operation, the period may be extended by parliament for a period not exceeding one year at a time and not extending in any case beyond a period of six months after the proclamation ceases to operate. The present Lok Sabha consists of 545 members.

Membership into Parliament

In order to be a member of parliament, a person must be a citizen of India and not less than 30 years of age in the case of the Rajya Sabha and not less than 25 years of age in the case of the Lok Sabha.

Functions and Powers of Parliament

As in other parliamentary democracies, the Indian parliament has the following functions: legislation; overseeing administration; passing of budget; airing public grievances; and debating various issues such as plans for development, international relations and national policies.

The distribution of power between the union and the states emphasises in many ways the general predominance of the Indian Parliament in the legislative field. Parliament has the power to legislate and amend the constitution. Parliament can, under certain circumstances, assume legislative power and exercise control over a subject that falls within the sphere exclusively reserved for the states. Parliament is also vested with the powers to impeach the president and to remove from office judges of the supreme court and high courts, the chief election commissioner, as well as the controller and auditor general in accordance with the procedures laid down in the constitution.

Administrative Setup

The Indian government's business is transacted in the ministries, departments, secretariats and offices. Allocation of the business among ministers is made by the president on the advice of the prime minister. The president may assign one or more departments under the charge of a minister. A cabinet minister is often assisted by a minister of state. Each department has an officer designated as secretary to the Indian government to advise the minister on policy matters and general administration.

The cabinet secretariat has an important coordinating role in decision making at the highest level. It operates under the direction of the prime minister. Its functions include submission of cases to the cabinet and its committees, preparation of records on decision taken and follow-up action on implementation. The cabinet secretariat also serves a committee of secretaries, which meets periodically with the cabinet secretary as head to consider and advise on problems requiring inter-ministerial consultation and coordination. The cabinet secretariat formulates the rules of business and allocates the business of the government to ministries and departments.

The Judiciary

The judiciary is modelled on the British form of jurisprudence and is independent of the executive and legislative arms of the government. At the apex of the judicial system is the Supreme Court of India, which consists of the chief justice and 25 judges of the supreme court. The president appoints the judges on the recommendation of the chief justice. The states have a high court with an elaborate and structured system of judges and magistrates for criminal and civil cases at different levels.

The judiciary is often considered the guardian of the nation. On many occasions, it has prosecuted even senior level ministers and bureaucrats. However, it has a huge backlog of cases, which can sometimes drag on for a long time.

Other than cases that drag on for years, another problem with the legal system is that the administrative machinery and paper work have not kept pace with the changing times. They continue to be many years behind the other areas of government. The current chief justice, Madan Mohan Punchhi, has initiated some moves to counter this problem. The Institute of Management Consultants in India has offered to support and provide honorary services to help improve the judicial and administrative systems. Computerisation is also underway in many courts to clear the backlog.

Indian Politics Then and Now

India has a multiparty political system that consists of national, regional and local parties. Jawaharlal Nehru formed the first government in post-independence India. As head of the Congress Party, he ruled India for almost 17 years. Nehru was succeeded by his daughter, Indira Gandhi. After Indira Gandhi's death, her son Rajiv Gandhi took over the reins of power. Thus, for most part of the period after independence, India was ruled by the Congress Party and the Nehru family.

Tragedy, however, struck the Gandhi family in more ways than one. In 1980, Indira Gandhi's politically active eldest son, Sanjay, was killed in a plane crash. In 1984, Indira Gandhi was assassinated by her bodyguards. In 1991, Indira's second son, Rajiv Gandhi, who was sworn in as her successor following her death, was killed by a suicide bomber.

P.V. Narasimha Rao became prime minister after Rajiv Gandhi. Narasimha Rao and Finance Minister Manmohan Singh took bold new steps to open up the Indian economy. After the general elections of May 1996, India saw two prime ministers—Deve Gowda and Inder Kumar Gujral—from the multi-party United Front coalition supported by Congress from outside. This period saw continued reforms in the Indian economy, which included a reduction in taxes and import tariffs. A number of power projects was also cleared.

Since her husband's death, Sonia Gandhi, the Italian-born widow of Rajiv Gandhi, has been an important figure in the Congress Party. Some people believe that she could gain the popularity of the masses if she stood for election, her rallying point being the wife of the late Rajiv Gandhi and a member of the Nehru family. Initially rejecting offers to be a member of the Congress Party, Mrs Gandhi subsequently agreed to campaign for the Congress Party in the 1998 election. In May 1997, she enrolled herself as an ordinary member of the Congress Party, and in March 1998, she became president of the Congress Party.

Atal Bihari Vajpayee became prime minister after the mid-term elections of 1998. He led a coalition of many parties, with the Hindu nationalist BJP (Bharatiya Janata Party) as the major party. Under his rule, India conducted five nuclear tests in May 1998, for which the United States and other countries imposed economic sanctions. The country could lose up to $20 billion in US and international loans. The Indian government's answer to this reaction from the United States and other countries was that it was self-sufficient and could survive even with the sanctions. But according to Indian economists, the country's growth rate, which is already lagging behind, may be slashed by half. Also, since the early 1990s, successive governments in New Delhi have been wooing foreign investors. It is feared that some investors may now shy away, at least for a while.

CHAPTER 3

Taxation, Revenue and Labour Issues

The highest economic decision-making body in India is the National Development Council. It consists of the prime minister, the finance minister, officials of the Ministry of Finance, chief state ministers and members of the planning commission, which is the government's think-tank on economic development policy. In the 1950s, the government drew up a programme of five-year economic plans to increase India's industrial production and to boost its agriculture. The country is now into its ninth five-year plan.

The Reserve Bank of India

The Reserve Bank of India (RBI) is the country's central bank. It was established in 1934 and started operating from April 1935 as a shareholder bank. The bank became a nationalised institution on 1 January 1949. The RBI:

- Issues currency notes
- Has the power to regulate the banking system directly by the Banking Regulation Act of 1949
- Acts as an advisor to the government on all financial problems
- Acts as a banker for the central and state governments, commercial banks and financial institutions
- Manages the rupee public debts of the central and state governments and is the custodian of the country's exchange reserve

The commercial banking system consists of about 295 scheduled commercial banks and two non-scheduled banks. Foreign banks, which specialise in finance and foreign trade, also compete for a piece of the domestic business. Currently, there are 31 foreign banks operating in India.

Currency and Exchange Rate
The Indian rupee is divided into 100 paise or coins. There are 5, 10, 25 and 50 paise, as well as 1 rupee and 2 rupees and coins. The paper currency consists of the following denominations: 1, 2, 5, 10, 20, 50, 100 and 500. The official fixed exchange rate mechanism was withdrawn on 1 March 1993, so the rupee floats on a basket of currencies. It now has a single market exchange rate and is convertible.

Main Sources of Revenue
The main sources of central revenue are as follows:

- Excise duties levied by the central government and corporate tax
- Income and wealth tax
- Estate and succession duties on non-agricultural assets and property
- Revenue from railways, posts and telegraph
- Customs duties

The main sources of revenue from the states are as follows:

- Taxes and duties levied by the state governments
- Taxes shared by the central government
- Grants received from the central government

Direct Tax
The Income Tax Department administers a number of direct tax acts, such as the Income Tax Act of 1961; the Wealth Tax Act of 1957; the Gift Tax Act of 1958; the Estate Duty Act of 1953

(discontinued in respect of death on or after 16 March 1985); the Companies Profit Surtax Act of 1964 (discontinued from 1 April 1988); the Hotel Receipts Tax Act of 1980 (levy discontinued from 28 February 1982); and the Expenditure Tax Act of 1987.

Income Tax
The history of income tax in India goes back to the 1860s when it was first levied by the British. Thereafter, the Income Tax Act was amended in 1886, 1922 and 1961. Many of the current laws concerning income tax relate to the amendments made to the Income Tax Act of 1961. Major changes were made to the Income Tax Act in the period 1996–1997.

The Income Tax Act of 1961 covers such areas as the basis for charging income, exemption from income tax on the basis of computation of income, set-off of income, clubbing of income, deductions, permissible deductions and double taxation. There are also special categories like non-resident Indians and income on dividends, assessment procedures, collection and recovery, and penalty and prosecution.

In 1962, income tax rules were formulated to clarify some provisions of the act and to provide some methods for implementation. These too have simultaneously undergone changes with the implementation of the act. The Central Board of Direct Taxes, the highest body for mediation and regulation, also clarifies doubts on the act and rules.

Currently, the government is expected to re-write income tax laws completely in order to simplify the taxpaying and assessment procedures. Those with income exceeding Rs50,000 per annum will be required to pay income tax irrespective of their status as individuals, firms, partnerships, corporate entities or corporate societies. This is unless they are incorporated as charitable trusts and enjoy certain exemptions under the Income Tax Act or are non-resident Indians who fulfil certain conditions of absence.

The tax that an individual or firm pays is assessed on the basis of income earned during the financial year. To prevent instances of tax evasion, the assessment process has now been formally structured to meet common dates. The financial year for all individuals and firms is 1 April–31 March of the following year. The corresponding assessment year is the subsequent year, during which assessment is made for the previous year's operational income. For instance, the assessment year would be 1998–1999 for the accounting year 1997–1998. There are various provisions for deductions at levels based on the economic development policy and the personal taxation policy adopted by the Indian government. Agricultural income is exempt from income tax.

Customs Duties

Besides taxes paid by individuals and firms, customs and central excise duties are two other important sources of tax revenue for the central government. From a maximum of 300%–400%, customs duties have gradually been reduced to around 35%. They are expected to decrease further to an average of about 25%.

India, a member of the World Trade Organisation (WTO), is bound by the organisation's norms to reduce the customs tariffs on a variety of items. Successive budgets are dismantling the tariff walls, thereby bringing the country closer to WTO targets.

Customs duties and rates are specified according to the schedules attached to the Customs Tariff Act of 1975. They are amended from time to time. With the aim of reducing customs duties, the 1996–1997 budget made provisions for amendments to the act. Goods considered essential for national development have since enjoyed exemption from customs duties. These include food grains, fertilizers, medical drugs and essential equipment.

Changes in Rates of Customs Duties for Some Commodities

Commodities	Customs Duties [Increase (+), Decrease (-)]
1. General	50% to 40% [-]
2. Live animals	50% to 40% [-]
3. Edible fruit and nuts	50% to 40% [-]
4. Oil seeds, etc.	50% to 40% [-]
5. Fats and oils	40% to 30% [-]
6. Cocoa and cocoa preparations	40% to 30% [-]
7. Beverage, spirits and vinegar	50% to 40% [-]
8. Tobacco	50% to 40% [-]
9. Sulphur, cement, etc.	50% to 40% [-]
10. Mineral oils & products	20% to 10% [-]
11. Inorganic chemicals	40% to 30% [-]
12. Organic chemicals	40% to 30% [-]
13. Pharmaceutical products	40% to 30% [-]
14. Fertilizers	40% to 30% [-]
15. Photographic or cinematographic goods	30% to 25% [-]
16. Rubber, leather, wood pulp, paper, books	50% to 40% [-]
17. Silk	40% to 30% [-]
18. Wool	50% to 40% [-]
19. Cotton	50% to 40% [-]
20. Pearls, precious stones, gold etc.	50% to 40% [-]
21. Iron & steel	30%
22. Nickel & articles thereof	20% to 10% [-]
23. Aluminium & articles thereof	10% to 20% [+]
24. Machinery	25% to 20% [-]
25. Railway equipment	50% to 40% [-]
26. Aircraft & parts thereof	50% to 40% [-]
27. Instruments, apparatus and appliances	50% to 40% [-]
28. Clocks & watches & parts thereof	50% to 40% [-]
29. Arms & ammunition	50% to 40% [-]
30. Toys, games and sports requisites	30% to 25% [-]
31. Works of art	50% to 40% [-]
32. Medical equipment	30% to 20% [-]
33. Electronics, telecom and computer sector	30% to 20% [-]

Source: Customs Tariff, 1997–1998

Customs duties consist of basic duties at a scheduled rate. Additional countervailing duties are sometimes levied on imports in order to protect Indian industries from dumping by exporters. Changes to the 1996–1997 budget have reduced and eliminated some forms of customs duties. These changes are in line with the General Agreement of Tariffs and Trade (GATT) and the WTO requirements. The finance bill of 1997 has also made some clarifications and changes to the Customs Tariff Act of 1975 in regard to customs duties.

Goods and duties are categorised in detailed schedules. The chief administering official is the chief controller of imports and exports. Occasionally, goods imported for re-export are exempt from customs duties. Since exchange rates are not constant, the value of duties depends on the date the goods arrive into the country. In the event that goods are lost, pilfered or destroyed, the duties may be reduced. Detailed bills of entry, import manifestos and packing lists ensure proper record-keeping of imported goods.

To expedite clearance at the port, a bill of entry can be filed 30 days in advance of the expected date of arrival of the vessel or aircraft. For preferential duties claims, a certificate of origin of goods must be produced in addition to the clearance documents. Some goods are further subject to an import licence requirement.

In an attempt to simplify excise taxation, the 1994–1995 budget:

- Reduced the number of ad valorem rates by about half
- Reduced the dispersal rates in each tariff chapter
- Reduced the number of exemption notifications by about half
- Shifted the bulk of excise taxation from specific to ad valorem rates to ensure built-in buoyancy of revenues
- Continued the lowering of unduly high rates
- Removed complicated price list procedures
- Extended MODVAT (Modified Value Added Tax) to capital goods, petroleum goods and spun yarns

The Tax Reform initiated in the 1996–1997 budget called for a simplification of the tax structure and a movement towards moderate rates of taxation.

The customs tariff reforms in the 1996–1997 budget:

- Substantially reduced duties on key raw materials like steel and chemicals
- Reduced the maximum rate of customs duties to 65%, with the exception of passengers' baggage, liquor, dried grapes, almonds and ball and roller bearings
- Further reduced customs duties on capital goods to 25% as a means of boosting investment to help the domestic capital goods industry
- Reduced or removed anomalies like import duties that were higher on raw materials and components than on finished products
- Eliminated notification of the administration of customs duties; thus, reducing discretionary power and any possibility for disputes

Central Excise

Central Excise is one of the largest sources of revenue for the Indian government. The government has the power to impose any form of taxation on the basis of the constitution, and excise duties are put on goods as per the Central Excise Act of 1944.

Every class of taxable goods under the act must be registered before production begins. The duty is collected when goods are removed from the place of production. Documents pertaining to the goods are then inspected by the central excise officers.

Sales Tax

The sales tax is the most important source of revenue for the states. By the Central Sales Tax Act of 1956, tax is levied on the interstate sale of goods. The act empowers the state governments to collect and retain the proceeds of such a tax. However, tax rates vary from state to state. Sometimes, there is a difference of more than

10% in the price of a product manufactured in the various states. The difference is often a major determinant in locating a plant.

Changes in the Rates of Excise Duties for Some Commodities

Commodities	Excise Duties [Increase (+), Decrease (-)]
1. Mineral oils & products	18%
2. Fertilizers	18% [-]
3. Explosives, matches, etc.	20% to 18% [-]
4. Leather goods	25% to 18% [-]
5. Printed books etc.	20% to 18% [-]
6. Silk	20% to 18% [-]
7. Wool	10% to 8% [-]
8. Cotton	20% to 18% [-]
9. Ceramic products	30% to 25% [-]
10. Pearls, precious stones, gold, etc.	nil
11. Iron & steel	nil
12. Railway equipment	18% to 15% [-]

Source: Central Excise Tariff, 1997–1998

Octroi

The Entry tax or Octroi is levied by the municipality to raise funds for local utilities. It is specific to cities and is levied on goods entering the municipal limits of cities.

Labour Legislation in India

Issues of taxation and revenue are closely related to the welfare of the group they affect most—the working population. Bearing this in mind, labour legislation in India relates to the following:

- Trade unions
- Wages and non-wage benefits

- Maintenance of harmonious labour-capital relations and the settlement of industrial disputes
- Welfare of the working classes, including provision for housing, recreation, as well as other social and cultural opportunities

The Beginning

Europe's eighteenth century industrial revolution triggered worldwide industrialisation. In turn, technological changes from the industrialisation process that swept through India effected changes in the labour movement and in the nature of the country's labour problems.

The opening up of the world markets gave additional opportunities to traders and merchants who, with an accumulation of capital, started functioning as industrial capitalists. These entrepreneurs ushered in a new industrial order of large-scale production and modern machinery. The mass transfer of people from agriculture to industry, however, complicated the relationship between the agricultural and industrial sectors.

Prior to 1919, labour legislation in India was rudimentary, extending only to factories and mines. The setting up of the Royal Commission on Labour in 1929 resulted in a recommendation to lend greater weight to the conventions of the International Labour Organisation (ILO). In 1942, the Ministry of Labour established the Indian Labour Conference based almost exactly on the tripartite pattern of the ILO. The Indian Labour Conference meets annually to examine all aspects of the proposed labour legislation.

Besides the Tripartite Committee of the ILO, the ILO conventions meets every six months to make a detailed examination of a select list of conventions and recommendations. Although India has so far ratified only 21 of the 104 conventions, this number is not significant because some of the ILO conventions are not relevant to the prevailing conditions in India.

Factory Acts and the Trade Union Act of 1926

The Factories Act of 1948 regulates various aspects relating to safety, health and welfare of workers employed in factories. It prescribes a 48-hour week for adult workers and forbids the employment of children under 14 years of age. It also lays down the minimum standards of lighting, ventilation, safety and welfare services that employers must provide for workers.

The Minimum Wages Act (1948) applies to a large number of industries (both industrial and agricultural). The act requires the government to fix the minimum rates of wages payable to the workers, review them periodically and revise them when necessary. There have, however, often been difficulties in implementing the provisions of the act, especially in the agricultural sector.

The Indian government passed the Fair Wages Act in 1951. The act takes into account the needs of the industry in a developing economy, the requirements of social justice and the need for adjusting wage-differentials so as to provide workers with incentives for advancing their skills. However, there are difficulties involved in determining an industry's "capacity to pay" as well as in measuring the productivity of labour. These tasks are complicated by the rationalisation of industries and the introduction of technological improvements.

Other acts applicable to any factory/business setting up shop in India are the Payment of Bonus Act, Employees Provident Fund Act, Payment of Gratuities Act, Workmen's Compensation Act and the Maternity Benefits Act.

Acts of Dispute

The Trade Disputes Act of 1929 provided for the setting up of Courts of Enquiry and Conciliation Boards. In addition, the act contains provisions for public utility services, such as railways, posts, telegraphs, telephones, undertakings that supply light or water to the public and any system of public conservancy or sanitation. The act seeks to check strikes and lockouts, helping

The majority of rural workers in India are poor and earn a salary that is barely enough to feed their families. Some of these workers do not enjoy any benefits from their employers.

both employers and employees formulate their respective cases before the lockout or strike is declared. The act was amended and its scope widened in 1938.

Other important acts of the pre-independence era are the Bombay Trade Disputes Conciliation Act of 1934 and the Bombay Industrial Disputes Act of 1938. By the Essential Services Ordinance of 1941, the Defence of India Rules 81A (1942) limits the liberty of workers to go on strike in certain sensitive industries like public transport and defence.

The Industrial Disputes Act of 1938 provides for the appointment of conciliation officers to act as mediators in trade disputes in order to promote settlement. The Industrial Disputes (Appellate Tribunal) Act (1950) makes provision for the establishment of a Central Appellate Authority to hear appeals against the awards or decisions of industrial tribunals. The Labour

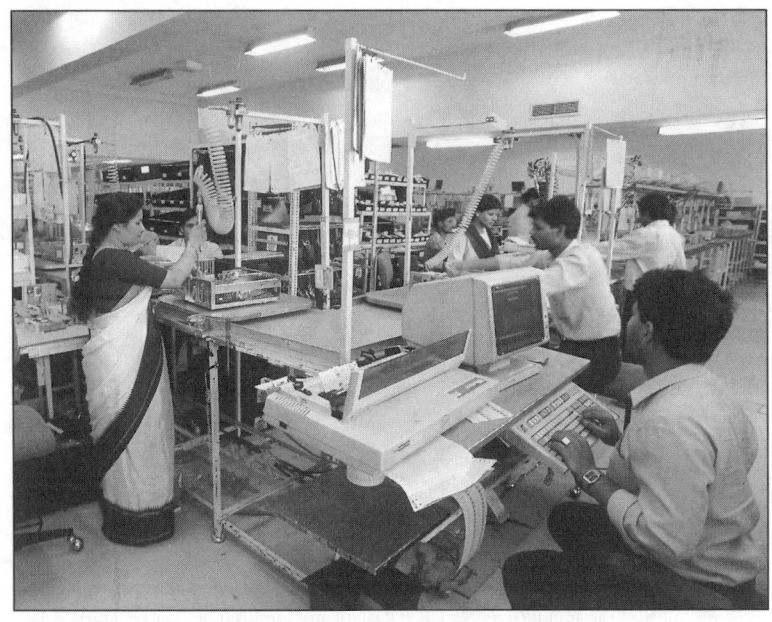

Indian women, unlike their counterparts of yesteryear, are educated and compete with men for jobs. More now have access to higher education.

Relations Act (1950) seeks to regulate the relationship between employers and employees. The act lays down the duties of the various authorities, as well as the rules of procedure and evidence.

The Industrial Disputes (Amendment and Miscellaneous Provisions) Act (1956) stipulates that "an award becomes enforceable on the expiry of 30 days from the date of its publication". The act is enforced by the government on the application of the concerned parties. Once the tribunal makes an award, it becomes effective for the purpose of its enforcement. According to a decision by the Lordships of the Supreme Court of India, an industrial tribunal has "all the trappings of a Court and performs functions which cannot but be regarded as judicial". The

Industrial Employment (Standing Orders) Act (1946) and the Industries (Development and Regulation) Act (1951) help ensure industrial peace. Profit sharing and labour co-partnership are other ways of ensuring industrial peace.

Workers' Welfare

The Bombay Central Provinces Act and the Madras Maternity Benefit Act of 1929, 1930 and 1935 deal with different areas of workers' welfare, such as education, medical aid, maternity benefits, recreation, housing, co-operative societies, grain and cloth shops, tea shops and canteens. Other acts that make provisions for facilities that enhance labour welfare are the Workmen's Compensation Act (1923); the Indian Dock Labourers Act (1934 and 1938); the Bombay Industrial Relations Act (1946); the Mica Mines Labour Welfare Fund Act (1946); the C.P. and Berar Industrial Disputes Settlement Act (1947); the Dock Workers Regulation of Employment Act (1948) the Coal Mines Provident Fund and Bonus Schemes Act (1948); the Employees' State Insurance Act (1948); the Bombay Housing Board Act (1949); the Madhya Pradesh Housing Board Act (1950); and the Factories Act of 1881.

Various amendments and enactments to the acts ensure protection for workers. Today, one of the key issues that the government has to tackle is the "exit policy", which gives an industry that has been taken over or a "sick" industry the power to lay off or retrench workers. This is a sensitive issue that sees the government time and again postponing its decision, owing to the "vote bank" potential of workers.

Social Security Measures

Social security, with its modern systematised forms of social assistance and social insurance, is a recent development in India. The term itself was authoritatively used only in 1935 when the

United States Social Security Act was enacted. Although there is no formal social security as such in India, a welfare system exists in the form of a subsidised supply of essential products for the poorer sections of society.

CHAPTER 4

Government Policy on Foreign Direct Investment

The policy of the federal government greatly influences the form and magnitude of foreign direct investment in a country. The Indian government, for one, has come up with a wide range of policies in regard to foreign direct investment since the country's independence in 1947. The policies have generally been in accordance with the government's developmental objectives.

The Industrial Policy Resolution (April 1948) recognised the role of foreign capital in India's efforts at industrialisation. There was, however, a need to regulate foreign capital into the country. A call was made for legislation to regulate such capital. Legislation was expected to ensure that majority ownership and effective control of all industries remained in the hands of Indians. However, in the foreign investment policy statement (April 1949), the government showed no intention of adopting any legislation to regulate foreign capital.

Foreign investment was encouraged on mutually advantageous terms. Although majority ownership of industries by the Indians was preferred, it was not the rule. Foreign investors were assured of the same treatment as local firms—unrestricted remittances of profits and dividends and fair compensation in cases of acquisition. Domestic firms, however, resented the equal treatment accorded to foreign investors. Local enterprises, for instance, found it difficult to compete with their foreign rivals in the consumer goods industry. They wanted foreign enterprises only in sectors where Indians lacked the technological expertise and general capability.

The Period 1950 to 1970

The Industrial Policy Resolution (April 1956) was drawn up in accordance with the goal of a "socialist pattern" of society as envisaged by the parliament in 1954. The resolution earmarked a number of important industries for the public sector, thereby reducing the scope of operation of local as well as foreign companies in the private sector. The resolution did not distinguish between domestic and foreign firms in the private sector.

Corporate taxes on income and royalties were reduced in the 1959 and 1961 budgets. To lower the tax burden of foreign investors, double taxation avoidance agreements were signed with most of the source countries, namely the United States, Sweden, Denmark, Japan and the erstwhile West Germany. India received a number of Western industrial and trade missions and sent industrial missions abroad in order to attract foreign capital into the country. The Indian Investment Centre, with offices in major investor countries, was set up in 1961 to promote foreign investment in India.

Western multinationals' response was cool in the early 1950s. In the period 1957 to 1967, however, substantial foreign investment flowed in. It was during this period that foreign drug firms set up a number of manufacturing subsidiaries in India.

The Period 1970 to 1990

In the next decade, 1968 to 1978, the outflow on account of remittances of dividends, profits, royalties and technical fees grew sharply and was a significant portion of the foreign exchange outflow of the country. As a result of a foreign exchange crisis in the late 1960s, the government streamlined procedures for foreign collaboration approvals and adopted a more restrictive stand in this area.

Following the recommendation of the Mudaliar Committee, a new agency called the Foreign Investment Board (FIB) was set up in 1968 to deal with all cases involving foreign investment or collaboration. A sub-committee of the FIB was empowered to approve cases of foreign collaboration where the proportion of foreign-held equity did not exceed 25% and where the total equity investment was up to Rs10 million. Administrative ministries were authorised to approve cases involving purely technical collaboration. Cases in which the total investment in share capital exceeded Rs20 million and where the proportion of foreign equity exceeded 40% were referred to the cabinet committee. Foreign investments unaccompanied by technology were not favoured.

The government's industrial policy of 1970 and 1973 imposed further restrictions on the activities of foreign companies and big local industrial houses. Core industries of "basic, critical and strategic importance" were specifically set aside for the government/public sector.

The Foreign Exchange Regulation Act (FERA) of 1973 attempted to tighten the laws concerning foreign exchange and transactions indirectly affecting it. All companies incorporated under the Indian Companies Act of 1956 with more than 40% foreign equity participation qualified under the act.

Companies that were in operation when FERA came into effect on 1 January 1974 were required to obtain the permission of the Reserve Bank of India (RBI) to continue functioning. Permission was subject to the Indianization or dilution of their foreign equity as per the guidelines of the government. These guidelines required foreign firms to transfer all their businesses to their Indian counterparts. Rupee (Indian) companies were also directed to dilute their foreign equity to a maximum of 40%.

FERA allowed only a select group of companies engaged in specified activities to have more than 40% foreign equity. Only these companies were given differential treatment by the Industrial Licensing Policy of 1973. The Industrial Policy Statement of 1977 declared that all other companies incorporated in India with up to 40% foreign equity would be free to expand, diversify and operate in any field like any other local company.

Workers in a tea plantation in India. Tea is a chief cash crop besides cotton, sugercane, coconuts, spices, jute, tobacco, coffee and rubber.

The Indianization of foreign firms brought about a significant change in the organisational structure of the foreign-controlled sectors of the economy. One important outcome was that all companies operating in the country (except foreign airlines, shipping and banking companies) were incorporated under the Indian Companies Act of 1956, thereby putting an end to the repatriation of "head-office expenses" by foreign firms. This provision had a significant effect on the tea plantation industry, which was dominated by over a hundred British tea companies.

Since the reorganisation, the business of foreign firms has been taken over by companies incorporated in India with as much as 74% foreign equity. Foreign firms with branch offices set up in India to monitor investment opportunities and oversee their investments had to pack up and leave. Except in the services sector, the "branch" as a form of operation by foreign companies came to an end.

Furthermore, of the nearly 900 companies that sought the permission of the RBI to continue their business, only about 150 (including tea companies) were permitted to retain higher levels of foreign equity. These companies alone remained outside the ambit of FERA. Others diluted their foreign equity to 40% as per the directives of the RBI. By complying, these companies gained the freedom to operate, expand and diversify in any industry open to local private firms.

The required dilution of foreign equity to 40% did not, however, mean that the companies in question ceased to be foreign-controlled. First, the criterion of 40% share holding was arbitrary. Effective control over a joint stock company can sometimes be exercised with as little as 10% block share holding. Both the Monopolies and Restrictive Trade Practices Act (MRTP) and the RBI regard the 25% equity holding to be adequate for exercising effective control. Secondly, FERA dilutions were effected in most cases not by the sale of foreign-held shares to Indian nationals but through the issue of fresh shares to Indian nationals This process of share allotment ensured that the new share holdings were widely dispersed. In addition, the clauses inserted in the Articles of Association just before the dilution of the shares gave special rights to foreign share holders. Therefore, the dilution of foreign share holdings did not necessarily imply a reduction in foreign management control.

When Rajiv Gandhi became prime minister in 1984, many reforms were expected to take place. Unfortunately, only a few did. In the telecommunications sector, the use and application of computers was liberalised, and technology missions were set up to accelerate economic growth and development. The car project Maruti entered into a partnership with Suzuki Motors of Japan.

Post–1991 Liberalisation

Major liberalisation took place only after the 1991 crisis, when the Indian government faced a major balance of payments problem. The International Monetary Fund (IMF) approved lending and recommended some measures for economic reforms. These were implemented. The reforms covered all areas of the economy, such as taxation and import duties (which were to be reduced), foreign direct investment (liberalisation in the rules relating to this), and the public sector (disinvestment in this sector).

When the New Industrial Policy (NIP) was implemented in 1991, India made serious efforts to accelerate the process of liberalisation and international competitiveness. A liberalised trade policy and reforms in the monetary and fiscal sectors sparked a comprehensive programme of economic reforms. These aimed at bettering India's macro-economic management for a fuller realisation of the country's vast economic potential.

The New Industrial Policy: A Closer Look

An important element of the NIP and the reform programme is the positive approach taken towards foreign investment and technology tie-ups, which are designed to attract capital inflows into the country. Foreign equity totalling 100% is now permitted in several sectors, while foreign investment totalling 51% in 36 high priority areas is automatically approved by the RBI within a few weeks of application.

The main thrust of the NIP is to enhance the competitiveness of the Indian economy and to globalise the country's foreign trade by providing greater transparency and a simplified procedural framework. Licensing requirements for industrial inputs have been removed. This means free access to capital goods, raw materials and spares.

Other important features of the NIP:

- Excluding a list of imports, the import and export of all industrial inputs are permitted.
- Significant reduction in import duties, ranging from nothing to 85%. Most capital goods attract a tariff that ranges between 20% and 40%.
- A number of special incentives given to exporters.

Protests: Two Cases

In Bangalore, angry farmers protested when the first Kentucky Fried Chicken (KFC) opened in the mid-1990s. They feared the restaurant would threaten their business and livelihood. Others protested on the grounds that fast food was an intrusion of Western culture into India. However, the protests did not last long. Indians soon embraced fast food culture. In fact, the controversy now seems worlds away, as children eat, drink and party in the special "party area" set aside in KFC restaurants.

In another case, Enron, one of the biggest power projects in India, ran into a plethora of problems. Although the power project was approved in 1992 by the local Congress government in Maharashtra, it was rejected in 1994 by the Shiv Sena-BJP government that came to power in the state. Also, because the local population had to make way for the project, groups who championed the cause of the local population protested, as did environmental groups.

Rebecca Marks, president of Enron, spent many months negotiating with the government for the project to take off. She also put her case forward to the government agencies and negotiated directly with the chief minister of the state. The project was finally approved in 1995.

An important lesson drawn from the Enron case is that sometimes, getting governmental approval for big projects, a hurdle in itself, is not enough. What is also important is to gain the trust of people who are going to be affected by the project. For instance, the "victims" could be made aware of the advantages of the new project such as the creation of new jobs. Also, in this case, the people involved in the project could have tried to explain to the local population how power generation would help accelerate the overall economic development of their state.

Main Sources of Foreign Direct Investment

There has been a surge in foreign direct investment in India from the United States, the United Kingdom, Japan and Germany. The huge leap in FDI figures for Mauritius (see table below) in 1995 compared to 1994 reflects a corporate structuring advantage. A double taxation avoidance agreement between India and Mauritius signed on 8 August 1982 resulted in a nil-tax for companies incorporated in Mauritius, thus attracting an inflow of investment. Other countries that have invested substantially in India include Hong Kong and Switzerland. Non-Resident Indians too make sizeable investment contributions to India both in the manufacturing and stock market sectors.

Foreign Direct Investment (1991–1995)

	Country	1991	1992	1993	1994	1995
1.	U.S.A.	325.09	1171.18	4785.00	3357.47	6534.43
2.	U.K.	497.64	759.52	2324.55	4275.51	1746.35
3.	Germany	553.75	580.37	401.18	1303.10	2378.35
4.	Mauritius	—	—	37.50	903.43	16462.96
5.	Japan	75.70	75.70	720.69	684.98	2180.60
6.	Italy	31.58	31.58	34.35	55.24	323.45
7.	Australia	—	—	0.19	23.98	321.47
8.	Singapore	—	—	114.97	13.37	2486.20
9.	Netherlands	153.65	153.65	148.44	1131.04	1414.95
10.	Hong Kong	12.67	12.67	129.25	251.64	3358.96
11.	Korea (South)	—	—	83.89	69.25	503.07
12.	Russia	—	—	—	—	2.50
13.	France	140.42	140.42	265.74	293.39	—
14.	Denmark	12.44	12.44	4.97	36.01	767.18
15.	U.A.E.	—	—	7.50	7.24	34.44
16.	Austria	5.93	5.93	34.58	15.06	36.72
17.	Bahamas	—	—	22.68	1.70	5.75
18.	Bahrain	4.84	—	—	17.53	8.95
19.	Belgium	—	20.10	24.69	76.74	67.42
20.	Bermuda	—	42.67	12.53	9.90	190.97
21.	Brazil	—	—	—	—	22.97
22.	British Virgin Islands	—	1.20	1.20	14.65	46.50
23.	Bhutan	—	—	—	19.0	—
24.	Canada	—	—	14.37	3.01	60.18
25.	Channel Islands	—	20.00	—	—	14.70
26.	China	—	1.35	—	—	0.18

	Country	1991	1992	1993	1994	1995
27.	Cyprus	—	—	—	—	3.25
28.	Czechoslovakia	—	—	17.00	—	0.70
29.	Finland	—	105.30	29.01	14.51	111.830
30.	Hungary	—	—	—	—	1.78
31.	Ireland	—	0.89	8.98	75.52	5.60
32.	Israel	—	—	6.51	6.22	26.89
33.	Iran	—	240.61	35.40	—	70.00
34.	Kuwait	—	—	0.44	2.47	—
35.	Luxembourg	—	46.46	—	—	64.84
36.	Liechtenstein	1.48	—	—	—	1.24
37.	Malaysia	—	—	3.11	157.24	218.41
38.	Norway	—	3.33	1.91	86.32	3.52
39.	Oman	0.87	—	0.05	40.00	33.59
40.	Panama	18.48	58.58	6.50	4.80	—
41.	Philippines	—	27.50	22.50	130.22	116.08
42.	Poland	0.40	—	—	3.10	
43.	Saudi Arabia	2.13	20.00	12.60	5.01	8.91
44.	South Africa	0.01	—	—	—	—
45.	Spain	_	—	22.05	11.02	0.82
46.	Sri Lanka	0.01	0.5	0.01	54.06	—
47.	Sweden	3.81	59.92	415.41	150.89	498.34
48.	Switzerland	1.53	547.03	1072.03	818.76	219.38
49.	Taiwan	3.12	3.00	9.15	115.35	91.89
50.	Thailand	—	—	—	117.93	144.13
51.	Ukraine	—	—	—	—	4.02
52.	West Indies	—	—	—	—	4.02
53.	Estonia	—	—	—	—	0.31
54.	NRI from various countries	1602.50	1496.90	5807.01	11565.50	19697.60
55.	All countries including above	66.21	1.27	63.72	422.84	1105.18
	Grand Total	3514.26	6751.80	17858.50	29716.50	63693.60

Source: India Development Report, 1997

Managers and supervisors communicate to their subordinates the need to manufacture products of the highest quality.

Towards Globalisation

The Indian government has also taken other steps to hasten its integration into the global economy. Market forces now determine the exchange rate of the rupee. Restrictions on foreign exchange transactions have also been relaxed. Foreign exchange is now freely available for such purposes as payment of royalties, lump sum fees, dividends and business development abroad. From 1991 until now, measures taken to open up Indian capital markets to overseas investors have included the following: the entry of Foreign Institutional Investors (FIIs) into the capital market, the promotion of foreign investment in offshore funds by Indian financial institutions and permission given to Indian companies to float Global Depository Receipts (GDRs) traded on major international stock exchanges.

The New Business Environment

Changes to the business environment include delicensing, deregulation and a bigger role for the private sector, which can now operate in all areas except those of strategic concern such as defence, railways and atomic energy. The list has been further pruned to permit private initiative in parts of the railway and transport sectors, as well as in mining, oil exploration and the oil refining and marketing sectors. The requirement of obtaining an industrial licence for manufacturing activity is now limited to only 16 industries of strategic, social or environmental concerns. All other industries in the metropolitan areas are exempt from licensing and are subject only to restrictions on location.

No Need to Panic: India's Safe

The contagion effect of Asia's currency crisis (1997 onward), domestic political uncertainty before Prime Minister Atal Behari Vajpayee came to power in early 1998 and the country's testing of nuclear weapons under Vajpayee's leadership have had their impact on India. The confusing signals sent by the Vajpayee government in the 1998 budget did not help matters either—the stock market bore the brunt of it. There has also been a dip in the exchange rate. In April 1998, the rate was Rs39 rupee to one US dollar. It went up to Rs42.50 in early September 1998. However, it is unlikely that India will face the same kind of crisis that countries in Southeast Asia are currently experiencing. The Indian economy has sound fundamentals. The country's forex reserves, for instance, are reasonably healthy at around US$30 billion. India is likely to maintain a growth rate of between 5% and 7% over the next 10 years.

Bureaucracy Reduced

Procedures leading to the approval of foreign investment have been streamlined. Proposals that satisfy specified conditions are given automatic approval by the RBI. They are reviewed by the Secretariat for Industrial Approvals (SIA) or the Foreign Investment Promotion Board (FIPB) based in the prime minister's office. The FIPB and SIA were set up specifically for the purpose of speeding up the approval process. Proposals involving investments totalling Rs3 billion are cleared by the finance minister, while those exceeding Rs3 billion are forwarded to the Cabinet Committee on Foreign Investment (CCFI) headed by the prime minister.

Foreign Exchange Controls Relaxed
Government control over disinvestment of equity by foreign investors has been relaxed. Such disinvestment is now permitted at market price for listed shares. Approval of the RBI is required for the disinvestment price of unlisted shares.

Participation in Capital Markets
FIIs have been given the go-ahead to invest both in the primary and secondary Indian capital markets, while Indian companies have been given permission to issue GDRs to allow international investors to participate in these markets. Offshore funds promoted by leading Indian financial institutions also present international investors the opportunity to enter Indian capital markets.

Foreign Investment in Trading Companies
The RBI automatically approves foreign investment of up to 51% foreign equity for new companies on the following basis: the company registers itself with the Ministry of Commerce (Office of DGFT) as an exporter/importer. The provisions of the prevailing EXIM (Export-Import policy of 1995–1996) allow the repatriation of dividends only after the company has registered itself with the Ministry of Commerce (Office of DGFT) as an export/star/super star trading house.

Where existing companies already registered as export/ trading/star/super star trading houses are concerned, the RBI approves foreign investment of up to 51% foreign equity after an application is made. Approval is subject to certain requirements.

Transactions at the Market Exchange Rate
All export and import transactions are now conducted at the market exchange rate. Similarly, all other foreign exchange transactions, including the inflow of foreign equity for investment, outflow in the event of disinvestment, payments in respect of repatriation of dividends, lump sum fees and royalties for technical know-how agreements and foreign travel, correspond to the market rate.

Investor Protection
Since January 1994, India has been a signatory to the Multilateral Investment Guarantee Agency (MIGA). The agency, set up by the World Bank, provides overseas businesses protection against political risks.

Clearance for Importing Capital Goods
The Export-Import policy envisages automatic clearance for importing capital goods provided the foreign exchange requirement for such imports is ensured through foreign equity.

The import of components, raw materials, intermediate goods and payment of know-how fees and royalties will be governed by the general policy applicable to other domestic units, as it is the foreign exchange for payment on account of dividends, royalties and fees. Other remittances may be obtained at the market rate. The payment of dividends will be monitored through the RBI only in the case of the consumer goods industry. This is to ensure that outflows on account of dividend payments are balanced by export earnings over a period of time.

Convertibility Clause Defunct

The mandatory convertibility clause, which enables financial institutions to convert loans into equity, will no longer be applicable for term loans extended by them for new projects.

Changes in Foreign Technology Agreements

- Automatic approval will be given to foreign technology agreements in high priority industries totalling a lump sum payment of Rs1 crore. There will be a 5% royalty for domestic sales and an 8% royalty for exports, subject to total payments of 8% of sales over a 10-year period from the date of agreement or seven years from the start of production. The prescribed royalty rates are net of taxes and calculated according to standard procedures.

- Industries other than those in the list of high priority industries will receive automatic approval subject to the same guidelines as those above if no free foreign exchange is required for any payment.

- All other proposals require specific approval under the general procedures in force.

- It is unnecessary to seek special permission to hire foreign technicians or for foreign testing of indigenously developed technologies. Payment may be made from blanket permits of free foreign exchange in accordance with the guidelines of the RBI.

A New Dimension in Public Sector Undertakings

While the public sector will continue functioning in select areas, the government will ensure that it is run on sound economic principles and that it continues to innovate and maintain its dominant role in strategic areas. Public sector investments will be reviewed towards this end. While some industries will be reserved for the public sector, no bars will be placed on these industries to be opened up to the private sector selectively. The public sector will also be allowed to enter areas previously not reserved for it.

In order to maximise resources and encourage wider public sector participation, part of the government's shareholding in the public sector will be offered to mutual funds, financial institutions, the general public and workers. "Chronically sick" public enterprises that are unlikely to turn around independently will be referred to the Board for Industrial and Financial Reconstruction (BIFR) or other similar high-level institutions for the formulation of revival or rehabilitation schemes. A social security mechanism will be created to protect the interests of workers likely to be affected by such rehabilitation packages.

Amendment to the MRTP Act
The Monopolies and Restrictive Trade Practices (MRTP) Act has been amended to remove the threshold limits of assets in respect of MRTP companies and dominant undertakings (companies that dominate the economy). Emphasis has been placed on controlling and regulating monopolistic, restrictive and unfair trade practices.

Liberalised Industrial Licensing Policy
Industrial licensing has been abolished for all industrial undertakings, including MRTP/FERA companies, except for industries with strategic, security, social and overriding environmental concerns, as well as those dealing in hazardous chemicals and items of elitist consumption. Industries reserved for the small-scale sector may continue enjoying their reserved status.

Areas where security and strategic concerns predominate may continue to be reserved for the public sector. In regard to projects requiring imported capital goods, automatic clearance will be given

- In cases where foreign exchange availability is ensured through foreign equity.

• If the CIF (Cost Insurance Freight) value of imported capital goods required is less than 25% of the total value (net of taxes) of the plant and equipment. For automatic clearance to apply, the CIF value must also be less than or equal to Rs2 crore.

In locations other than cities with a population of more than one million, there is no requirement to obtain industrial approvals from the central government (except for industries subject to compulsory licensing). In cities with a population greater than one million, industries other than those of a non-polluting nature, such as electronics, computer software and printing, must be located 25 km from the periphery unless situated in designated industrial areas.

In cities with a population greater than one million and requiring industrial re-generation, a flexible location policy will be adopted for industrial plants. Zoning the Land Use Regulation and Environmental Legislation will continue regulating industrial locations. Land is zoned according to purpose of usage, which may be agricultural, industrial, commercial or residential.

Appropriate incentives and investments in infrastructural development will help reduce congestion in the cities and promote the dispersal of industries, particularly to the rural and economically backward areas.

The Foreign Investment Promotion Board

In order to increase foreign direct investment into India, the government reconstituted the FIPB in 1995. The board consists of a core group of secretaries to the government. It also consists of top officials from financial institutions and banks, as well as experts from the industrial sector.

Objectives and Functions of the FIPB

One of the objectives of the FIPB is to promote foreign direct investment into India by undertaking investment promotional activities. The FIPB also facilitates the investment needs of international companies, non-resident Indians and other foreign investors in projects considered beneficial to the Indian economy. The board considers all investment proposals with or without technical collaboration and/or industrial licence.

The main functions of the board are:

- To ensure expeditious clearance of proposals for foreign investment
- To review periodically the implementation of the proposals previously cleared by it
- To review the policy relating to foreign direct investment and in consultation with other concerned agencies, evolve a set of transparent guidelines for facilitating foreign investment in various sectors
- To undertake investment promotional activities that include establishing contact and inviting a select group of international companies to invest in appropriate projects
- To interact with the Industry Associations/Bodies and other government and non-government agencies on relevant matters in order to facilitate an increased inflow of foreign direct investment into the country
- To identify sectors into which investment may be sought, keeping in view the national priorities and also the specific regions of the world from which investment may be brought in through special efforts
- To undertake all other activities for promoting and facilitating foreign direct investment as and when necessary

Procedures of the FIPB

The FIPB meets on specific days every week to ensure quick disposal of the cases on hand. It has more frequent meetings whenever these are deemed necessary.

Foreign investment proposals received by the board's secretariat must be shown to the board within 15 days of their receipt. Administrative ministries must offer their comments either prior to and/or during the meeting of the FIPB. The FIPB must ensure that, as far as possible, the government's decisions on a foreign direct investment proposal are communicated to the applicants within six weeks.

The board must have the flexibility of purposeful negotiation with the investors and should consider project proposals in their totality, free from parameters, in order to ensure maximum foreign direct investment into the country. The FIPB must function as a transparent, effective and investor-friendly single window to provide clearance for foreign investment proposals. The board must lay down its own mode of operation, keeping in view the requirements of every proposal it considers.

Approval Level

The recommendations of the FIPB with respect to project-proposals, each involving a total investment of Rs600 crore or less, will be considered and approved by the industry minister. The recommendations with respect to projects, each with a total investment of over Rs600 crore, will be submitted to the CCFI for a decision. The CCFI will consider the proposals referred to it as well as those rejected by the industry minister. The approval letters in all cases will be issued by the secretariat of the FIPB.

Secretariat of the FIPB

The secretariat of the FIPB is located in the Department of Industrial Policy and Promotion, Ministry of Industry. The secretariat receives and processes the applications/proposals for foreign investment and places them before the FIPB for consideration. Thereafter, it submits the recommendations of the board to the Ministry of Industry.

The secretariat ensures that all applications are presented to the FIPB within 15 days. The secretariat is also responsible for communicating to the applicants the final decisions of the government. In addition, the secretariat promotes and facilitates investment, as well as provides guidance and advice to entrepreneurs in the post-approval amendments stage.

Foreign Investment Promotion Council

The council has been constituted to undertake and coordinate vigorous promotional and marketing activities in regard to investment. This entails making extensive contact with potential investors, as well as lobbying and interacting with individual companies.

The council was set up as a result of the decision of the government to strengthen the institutional mechanism relating to the consideration and approval of foreign direct investment proposals. The council is also responsible for analysing requirements in the various sectors and industries in India that are in need of modernisation, technology upgrading and capital infusions.

The council has a two-pronged strategy. The first pertains to approvals and clearance required as per the transparent guidelines. The other relates to full-time promotional and marketing activities concerning investment. Accordingly, a revamped FIPB with fresh guidelines has been put under the direct control of the Industry Ministry, thereby reducing the decision-making process by one level. In short, the FIPC was set up to be proactive in outlook in regard to FDI and identify areas that can benefit from such investments.

Earlier efforts at foreign investment centred mostly on addressing general investment promotional seminars and conferences. A more target-oriented approach is now being adopted to identify the sectors/projects in the country that require foreign direct investment. The council also hopes to pinpoint the specific regions and countries from which foreign direct investment would be brought in through special efforts.

Invest in India Cell

An Investment Promotion & Project Monitoring Cell commonly known as Invest in India Cell was set up in the Department of Industrial Development in 1995. The cell is headed by a member-secretary from the SIA.

The Invest in India Cell attends to inquiries from entrepreneurs on a wide range of such subjects as licensing policy, tariff and duties, corporate taxation and company law. Officers have been placed in the Finance and Commerce Ministries, the RBI (New Delhi and Mumbai) and the Indian Investment Centre (New Delhi) to provide clarifications on certain matters. The Invest in India Cell schedules meetings with the officers concerned at the entrepreneur's request.

The cell also monitors the implementation progress of the various projects so as to facilitate approvals at the state government and other levels. Arrangements are being made to receive information from the state governments through a computer network so as to coordinate all approval processes with the National Informatics Centre (NIC).

General Permission for Foreign Technicians

The RBI has granted general permission to foreign technicians to render technical service in India pursuant to their engagement by a firm or a company in or resident in India. The firm or company must pay remuneration or a fee to the foreign technician pursuant to such an engagement. The firm or company must also remit the amount outside India through an authorised dealer, subject to certain conditions.

Special Permission for Foreign Technicians

Firms/companies intending to engage the services of foreign technicians on any other terms should apply to the RBI for permission by using the form EFN (Employment of Foreign Nationals). The form must be duly signed by the foreign technician for permission under Section 30 of FERA, 1973. However, in cases where the technical collaboration agreement provides for the deputation of technical and other personnel to whom no fees are payable, approval of the RBI is not required. Prior clearance by the Ministry of Home Affairs is required if the period for engaging a foreign technician exceeds three months.

Engaging Non-technical Foreign Personnel
Indian firms proposing to engage non-technical foreign personnel on payment of fees should apply to the Administrative Ministry of the Indian government irrespective of the period of engagement. On receipt of government approval applications, the form EFN should be submitted to the RBI for formal permission under Section 30 of FERA, 1973.

Appointment of Foreign Nationals as Directors
In the case of foreign nationals who are appointed as directors of Indian companies—according to Section 269 of the Companies Act (1956)—the foreign nationals in question should submit their applications to the RBI (the form EFN) through companies in India for permission under Section 30 of FERA, 1973.

Applications for engaging foreign technicians other than those described above, foreign personnel other than technicians or foreign nationals as directors must be referred to the RBI (on the form EFN) for prior approval. Indian firms/companies intending to engage, on payment of fees, foreign personnel—whether technicians or otherwise—need not thereafter apply to the Administrative Ministry of the Indian government before submitting the application (the form EFN) to the RBI.

Indian Technicians for Training Abroad
Entrepreneurs who intend to send Indian personnel abroad for training and other purposes need only approach the RBI. Permission is easily obtainable.

Remittance of Dividends, Interest, Royalties and Technical Fees

Indian companies that have issued equity to non-resident shareholders are required to make payments of profits/dividends to non-residents in foreign exchange. In certain cases, Indian companies are required to obtain the approval of the RBI for remittance of dividends to non-residents in foreign exchange.

Indian companies are required to pay dividends to all their non-resident shareholders through normal banking channels. Such companies should apply to the RBI to remit dividends in a consolidated manner.

Remittance of Profits by Foreign Firms

With the exception of banks, profits earned in India by branches of foreign-incorporated foreign firms may not be remitted to their head offices overseas without the prior approval of the RBI. Applications for profit remittance must be made to the RBI through the applicant's bank by letter (in duplicate) along with the relevant documents. As long as their profits are derived from business conducted in India, local branches of foreign banks must apply to the RBI for net profit/surplus remittance to head offices outside India. Applications should be submitted, along with the relevant documents, after the accounts for the year in question has been finalised in accordance with the provisions of Section 29 of the Banking Regulation Act of 1949.

Remittance of Interest

Remittances on interest concerning the securities of the central or state governments in India, bank deposits held in India and dividends on units of the Unit Trust of India to individuals permanently residing outside India may be made by authorised dealers without the prior approval of the RBI, subject to certain conditions.

Refund of Income Tax to Non-resident Firms

Remittances on account of refunding income tax to foreign firms abroad require the prior approval of the RBI. Applications must be made on Form A2, supported by the relevant documents.

Increase in Applications and Relaxed Guidelines

The changes brought about in policies concerning foreign investment have evoked a strong positive response from foreign companies. The number of applications received for foreign investment has increased substantially and continues on an upward trend.

The requirement of prior government approval for direct overseas investment by Indian companies has also been relaxed—the guidelines set out in 1996 provide automatic approval within 30 days.

CHAPTER 5

Types of Business Enterprises

The main types of business organisations in India are as follows:

- Private and public companies
- Partnerships
- Sole proprietors
- Government companies
- Co-operative societies
- Charitable trusts

Companies

Companies incorporated in India and branches of foreign corporations are regulated by the Companies Act of 1956. The act is in many ways similar to the United Kingdom Act; however, the Indian Act is more restrictive.

A company refers to a business organisation formed and registered under the Companies Act of 1956 or any previous Companies Act. A corporate body includes both Indian and foreign companies, while a company refers to only an Indian company.

Companies incorporated under the Companies Act are limited liability companies with a share capital. Companies limited by guarantee or unlimited companies, though permissible, are rare. The provisions relating to disclosure, audit, record keeping, transparency of results announced in the newspapers and so on are more stringent in the case of public companies than private ones. A private company that is a subsidiary of a public company is treated as a public company.

There are three types of companies: public and private companies, partnerships and proprietary firms. A company may be incorporated either as a public or a private company. To qualify as a private company, its Articles of Association (bylaws) must:

- Restrict the right to transfer the company's shares
- Limit the number of shareholders to 50 (excluding employees and former employees)
- Prohibit any invitation to the public to buy shares or debentures

The Companies Act states that any company is deemed a public company if any of the following conditions are met:

- Twenty-five percent or more of its paid-up share capital is held by one or more corporate bodies.
- It holds 25% or more of the paid-up share capital of a public company.
- Its average annual turnover is above a prescribed amount.
- It accepts a deposit from the public after such an invitation for deposits is made public through an advertisement. It then renews its public deposits. Deposits from shareholders, directors and their relatives are not treated as public deposits.

Subsidiaries
A company is a subsidiary of its holding company if the following conditions are met:

- The composition of the board of directors is controlled by the holding company.
- The holding company controls more than half the total voting power in the subsidiary.
- The subsidiary is a subsidiary of any other company, which itself is the subsidiary of the holding company.

Formation Procedure

A certificate of incorporation is given after the required documents are presented, along with the requisite registration fee, to the Registrar of Companies. The required documents are as follows: a printed copy of the memorandum and the Articles of Association signed by each initial subscriber. The registrar must be satisfied that all other requirements have been complied with. A company becomes a legal entity as soon as it is granted the certificate of incorporation.

When a company is formed, its main expenses are as follows: the professional fees for drafting the memorandum and the Articles of Association, the cost of printing them and the fees paid to the Registrar of Companies. The registration fees paid to the registrar depend on the share capital of the company as stated in its memorandum. The minimum fee is Rs200 and the maximum Rs4 million.

Application for a Name

The time taken for a company to be incorporated is usually two to three months, after the proposed name of the company is approved by the Registrar of Companies. A formal application has to be made for such an approval. This is because the law requires that a company not be registered with any undesirable name or any name similar to that of an existing company. The formal application can be made at around the same time the memorandum and the Articles of Association are drafted.

The documents filed at the Registrar of Companies are available for public inspection. When registered, the memorandum and Articles of Association are binding on the company and its shareholders.

Capital Structure

There is neither any statutory limit to the amount of authorised share capital of a company nor is there any prescribed minimum amount of authorised capital. The maximum capital a company issues is limited by the authorised capital set out in its charter. If the bylaws permit, the amount of authorised capital may be increased. The share issued is called the issued capital, while the amount subscribed is called the subscribed capital. The amount paid is known as the paid-up capital.

Number of Shareholders

A private company must have a minimum of two shareholders as opposed to a minimum of seven shareholders for a public company. The maximum number of shareholders for a private company is 50. Since shares cannot be issued to a non-resident without the approval of RBI, the initial subscribers are almost always Indian nationals.

Kinds of Share Ownership

Shares are registered with a company, which has to keep a register of its members. Bearer shares cannot be issued without the approval of the central government.

Share Capital

There are two kinds of share capital. One is common stock called equity shares; the other is preferred stock called preference shares. Shares may be of any amount, but common stock must have a par value of Rs10 and the preferred stock a par value of Rs100. Each share must be distinguished by an appropriate serial number.

Preferred stock can be issued only if it is redeemable within 10 years and if authorised by the company's bylaws. These shares may only be redeemed out of profits that would otherwise be available for dividend or out of the proceeds of a fresh issue of shares made for the purpose of redemption. Holders of preferred stock do not have voting rights unless the preference dividends are in arrears.

Debentures and Loans

Debenture as used in the Companies Act includes debenture stock, bonds and other securities of a company, whether or not they constitute a charge on the company's assets. A debenture is normally issued as security for a loan and is an instrument executed under the seal of a company, charging the whole or part of its undertaking in favour of the holder to secure the sum loaned. It provides for the payment of interest at a specified rate until the repayment of the principal amount.

Debentures containing a charge must be registered with the Registrar of Companies. They are usually redeemable at a specified date, although the Companies Act permits the issue of irredeemable debentures. Terms of issue of debentures may also entitle the holder to convert them into shares under specific terms at specified times. Debentures are fully transferable and may be quoted on the stock exchange. A company issuing debentures must create a debentures redemption reserve in accordance with government guidelines.

Increasing Subscribed Capital

Subscribed capital can be increased to the limit of the authorised capital by the allotment of further shares. These shares must be offered in proportion to the number of existing shareholders unless otherwise decided at the company's general meeting. If the bylaws permit, a company may also increase the subscribed capital by the capitalisation of profits and issue bonus shares (stock dividends) in accordance with prescribed rules.

Stock dividends can be issued out of free reserves built from genuine profits or from share premiums collected in cash. They can be issued with the consent of the controller of capital issues. Guidelines have been laid down for the consideration of bonus issue proposals.

Some important legal requirements consist of provisions designed to ensure that the share capital remains intact; thus, a company may not pay a dividend out of capital. A reduction of capital, whether by refund to shareholders or otherwise, can only be made if sanctioned by the court, which has to be satisfied that the interests of creditors have been protected.

Transferability of Shares

A company may not buy its own shares. It may also not render any financial assistance, whether direct or indirect, in connection with the purchase of or subscription for any shares in its holding company (it may hold shares in its holding company only under certain circumstances). However, financial assistance by the company is permitted in some circumstances to enable the employees or their trustees to purchase or subscribe for its fully paid shares. "Buy back" of shares by companies is now pending the approval of the government. An announcement in regard to this is expected soon.

Shares may be issued at par value or at a premium or discount. The excess of the total issue price for shares over their par value must be transferred to a share premium account and disclosed as such under reserves and surplus. The premium may only be used for specific purposes as set out in Section 78 of the Companies Act. Shares can be issued at a discount provided they are of a class already issued, and the date of issue is more or less one year from the time the company was allowed to start business.

Shares may be transferred by submitting the share scrip and transfer document signed by the transferror and the transferee. The document must bear the right amount of stamp duty. Shares in companies are prima facie freely transferable unless the company's bylaws confer the power of refusal to transfer. A private company must include this power in its bylaws. In the case of quoted companies, the stock exchange listing requirements demand that the shares be freely transferable.

Transfer of shares to a non-resident, as stated earlier, can be effected only if it is permitted by the RBI. There are also certain restrictions, with an undertaking covered by the Monopolies and

Restrictive Trade Practices Act (an MRTP company), on the transfer of a company's shares. In broad terms, these restrictions are applicable to any person or group holding a prescribed percentage or more of the shares of the MRTP company. In the case of a company limited by shares, the liability of the shareholders is limited to the par value of the shares held by them.

Roles and Responsibilities of Directors

It is the directors' responsibility to conduct the business of a company. Directors are largely subject to the same laws as independent business persons, plus any law relating to the trade in which they are engaged. The obligations imposed on directors by company law include those designed to ensure that proper information about the company is made available to the general public and potential investors. Directors must take into account the interests of the employees and shareholders. Ultimately, they must also bear legal responsibility for the actions of the employees.

The power and duties of the directors are contained in the company's bylaws. The Companies Act also contains elaborate provisions for the power and duties of the board of directors, as well as the restrictions imposed on them. Every director who has an interest in a contract or arrangement entered into by the company must disclose the nature of his or her interest at a meeting of the board of directors. The company is then required to record the director's interest in a register, which is available for general inspection. It must be noted that a director is deemed to have an interest in a company only if he or she holds more than 2% of the shares of the company, individually or along with other directors.

The appointment and remuneration of a managing or full-time director or manager in a public or private company, which is a subsidiary of a public company, is subject to the approval of the central government by the Companies Act of 1956. This is unless such an appointment is made in accordance with the conditions and within the ceiling limits specified in Schedule XIII of the act, and a return is filed within 90 days from the date of such an appointment. There is no statutory requirement for a director to be the shareholder of a company. However, bylaws may require him or her to hold a specified number of shares known as share qualification.

The Companies Act permits the company to fix the period of appointment for up to one-third of the total number of directors, subject to certain provisions. The remaining two-thirds must be those directors who are liable to retire by rotation; of these, those who have been in office the longest since their last appointment must retire at the annual general meeting.

Every public and private company (which is a subsidiary of a public company with a paid-up share capital of Rs50 million or more) is required to have a full-time director or manager. Each company with a paid-up share capital of Rs2.5 million or more is required to have a full-time qualified secretary. When the board of directors of such a company consists of only two directors, neither of them may be the secretary of the company. Generally, there are no restrictions on the nationality of the board members.

A foreigner may be appointed as the director of a company, subject to government approval. He or she can also appoint someone to act for him or her if the company's articles permit this and if such an appointment is approved by the board of directors. It is also possible to provide for proportional representation when appointing directors.

The terms of appointment of expatriates as managing or full-time directors or managers have to be approved by the government. Under the law, a foreign managing director cannot be appointed for a period of more than five years at a time. Employee representation on the board of directors is not legally compulsory.

Meetings of Shareholders and Directors

Every public company with a share capital must hold a meeting of shareholders—called statutory meeting—every one to six months from the time it is entitled to commence business. The board of directors must forward a report called the statutory report to each shareholder of the company at least 21 days before the date of the shareholders' meeting, outlining particulars (the Annual Report that contains information about the company's performance in general and the financial performance in particular) as specified in the Companies Act.

An annual general meeting of shareholders must be held at least once every calendar year, and no more than 15 months may lapse between annual general meetings. However, the first annual general meeting may be held within 18 months from the date of incorporation of the company. Dates of subsequent general meetings may be extended by the Registrar of Companies by a maximum of three months.

Matters dealt with at the annual general meeting include the following: consideration of the company's accounts; directors' and auditors' reports; declaration of dividends; and appointment of new directors and auditors, as well as their remuneration package.

An annual return containing particulars, as specified in the Companies Act, must be filed at the Registrar of Companies within 60 days from the date of the annual general meeting. An extraordinary general meeting of shareholders may be called by the board of directors at the request of a specific number of shareholders.

The Companies Act stipulates that a meeting of the company's board of directors be held at least once every three months and that at least four such meetings be held every year. Minutes must be kept for the general meetings of shareholders and the meetings of the board of directors or their committees.

Every equity shareholder has the right to a ballot vote in proportion to his or her share of the paid-up equity capital of the company. However, when voting is done by a show of hands, every equity shareholder has the right to one vote for every shareholder present. No common stock can be issued with such proportional voting rights. Although entitled to notice of meetings, holders of preferred stock are not usually allowed to vote unless the preferred dividends are in arrears.

Dividends
No dividend may be declared except out of profits arrived at after providing the prescribed minimum amount of depreciation and after transferring a prescribed percentage of profits. The profits must not exceed 10% to reserve if the dividend declared exceeds 10%.

The rules seek to establish a relationship between dividends declared and the profits transferred to reserve. For instance, if a company transfers more than 10% of its profits to reserve, it must then ensure a prescribed minimum distribution of dividends. Also, the proposed amount transferred to reserve is restricted if no dividend is declared.

There are rules regulating the transfer of past reserves for the payment of current dividends. A brief evaluation surplus (a surplus arising from a revaluation of fixed assets) may not be used for payment of dividends in cash or for issue of a stock's dividends by way of bonus shares. However, an amount equivalent to the depreciation on the revaluation surplus may be transferred to an income statement.

Audit Requirements and Practices
Companies incorporated under the Companies Act must keep proper books and records that give an accurate reflection of the company's accounts and state of affairs.

Companies must appoint auditors at each annual general meeting. Among other matters, the auditors' report must declare whether the accounts give a true and fair picture of the state of affairs in the company and the results of its performance.

All companies whose annual turnover exceeds a specified amount must have a tax audit carried out in accordance with the provisions of the Income Tax Act of 1961. The government may direct cost audits to be carried out in companies, which are required to maintain detailed cost-accounting records.

Record-keeping Requirements

Every company is required to keep the following books of accounts:

- A cash and bank book to record matters concerning the receipts and expenses of the company
- A sales and purchase register of goods bought/sold/manufactured by the company
- An assets register

A company engaged in production, processing, manufacturing or mining activities must also keep such details of utilization as purchase/sales of material, labour costs and other items of cost prescribed by the government.

Accounting and Book-keeping Requirements

There is no provision in the Companies Act as to the way in which books of accounts are to be maintained, but it is incumbent on a company to maintain such books on a cash or accrual basis. Relevant books and vouchers have to be maintained for a period of at least eight years after the end of the financial year.

The books of accounts must be kept at the company's registered office. In the case of a company with a branch office, the books of accounts relating to the branch transactions may be kept at the branch office. If the board of directors decides to keep the books at a place other than the registered office, it must inform the Registrar of Companies within seven days of its decision and provide the address of the place where the books are located.

The books of accounts and other books and papers are open to inspection by any director of the company, the Registrar of Companies or any authorised government official during business hours. Shareholders have no right to inspect the books of accounts, except when the company winds up.

In addition to the books of accounts, a company is required to keep the following registers:

- An investment register
- A register of shareholders
- A register of directors and their shareholdings
- A minutes book of shareholders' and directors' meetings

Shareholders have right of access to these registers. The registers must be kept at the registered office of the company.

Audited Financial Statements

With every notice of the annual general meeting of a company, the board of directors must furnish shareholders with financial statements consisting of a balance sheet and a profit and loss account. These financial statements must be accompanied by the auditors' report and the report of the company's board of directors. The auditor is required to report on a list of matters prescribed in the Companies Act.

The period covered by the income statement should not end on a date more than six months before the date of the annual general meeting. This is so unless the date of the general meeting is extended by the Registrar of Companies. In the case of the first annual general meeting, the gap between the two dates may be nine months. The financial year should not exceed 15 months.

However, with special permission from the Registrar, this period may be extended to 18 months.

The audited financial statement, together with a report by the board of directors, must be sent to shareholders and trustees for debenture-holders at least 21 days before the date of the annual general meeting. However, this requirement may be dispensed with in the case of quoted companies if copies of these documents are made available for inspection at the annual general meeting. An abridged set of accounts in a prescribed form must also be sent to shareholders and trustees for debenture-holders. Quoted companies are also required by their listing agreement with the stock exchange to furnish results (financial statements) to the stock exchange on a half-yearly basis within two months of the expiry period. Many Indian companies now conform to international disclosure norms. The companies must make an announcement of their financial results in an English language newspaper.

A company that has subsidiaries must also submit the financial statements and investments, as well as the reports of the board and auditor of each subsidiary. All these statements and reports must be prepared in accordance with the requirements of the Companies Act. The time lapse between the balance sheet date of the holding company and the subsidiaries should not exceed six months.

After the accounts have been presented at the annual general meeting, three copies of these accounts, together with all the required documents attached (auditors' report, board's report, etc.), must be filed with the Registrar within 30 days of the date of the annual general meeting. The audited accounts have to be submitted to the tax authorities along with the income return.

Appointment of Auditors and Auditing Requirements

An accounting firm is usually appointed as the auditor of a company. Neither an officer nor an employee of a company nor a corporate body can be appointed as the auditor of the company. No person who is a partner or in the employment of an officer or employee of the company can be appointed as the auditor of that company.

The need for an independent auditor cannot be overemphasised. It is also considered improper for an auditor to have a financial interest in the company to which he or she reports. If, however, the auditor has a substantial interest—"20% of voting power"—in the company's finances, he or she is required to disclose this in his or her report.

According to the Companies Act, officers refer to the directors, company secretary and other employees of a company. The act sets a limit on the number of company audits that may be undertaken by an auditor. The ceiling is 20 companies per partner of an audit firm, of which companies with a paid-up share capital of more than Rs2.5 million should not number more than 10. The auditor has, at all times, the right of access to the accounting and other records of the company. He or she has the right to demand from the officers of the company such information and explanations as he or she deems necessary for the audit.

Tax Audit

It is necessary for every company with a total sales turnover or gross receipts of more than Rs4 million to have its accounts audited in accordance with the Income Tax Act. This audit is in addition to the statutory audit under the Companies Act. It mainly involves verification and confirmation of certain facts, figures and information generally required by the Income Tax authorities in the course of tax assessment proceedings.

The auditing practices broadly relate to checks on the following:

- Examination of books of accounts
- Methods of accounting employed and their consistency

- Methods of valuation and the quantitative reconciliation of inventories
- Amounts of expenditure incurred under various heads that are not allowable in full or that result in direct or indirect benefits to the directors, relatives or officers of the company
- Borrowings and repayments of certain types of loans
- Prior-period adjustments
- Deductions of tax at source

The above points have to be certified as true based on the auditors' opinion, and information and explanations received. The accounts of the company audited under the Companies Act, together with the documents forming part thereof, must be attached to the tax audit report.

The tax audit requirements also apply to other types of business entities whose total sales turnover or gross receipts in business exceed Rs4 million. They also apply to those business entities whose gross receipts exceed Rs1 million in any year with some variations.

Cost Audit

A company, required to maintain cost accounting records, may be directed by the government to have a cost audit conducted. Unlike the financial audit and tax audit carried out every year, a cost audit is carried out only at the specific order of the government. The cost auditor submits his report to the Company Law Board of the central government and sends a copy of the report to the company.

Liquidation/Receivership

Companies registered under the Companies Act can be terminated through a winding-up (liquidation), in which case their names are struck off the Registrar of Companies. Alternatively, in the case of an amalgamation, they may be dissolved without a winding-up. The winding-up of a company may be done voluntarily or subject to the supervision of the court.

A shareholder's voluntary winding-up requires a declaration of solvency by the directors. Otherwise, the winding-up becomes a creditor's voluntary winding-up. The winding-up provisions and the circumstance under which each mode of winding-up is undertaken are contained in part VII of the Companies Act. A liquidator is appointed to sell the assets and discharge the liabilities. If there is any surplus, he distributes them to the shareholders in accordance with their respective interests.

The Partnership Act

The law prohibits partnerships of more than 10 persons in the banking field and partnerships of more than 20 persons from doing any other business. Limited partnerships are not legally recognised in India.

The Indian Partnership Act of 1932 contains provisions for the voluntary registration of firms with the Registrar of Firms. Although not compulsory, registering a partnership ensures certain legal rights to the firm and its partners.

Formation Procedure

A partnership is formed by an agreement among the concerned partners to share the profits of a business. The agreement need not be in black and white, but it is advisable to have one done.

A partnership is relatively simple to form, and formation costs are inexpensive. A corporate boss may also be a partner. A partner may be a foreigner if specific permission is obtained from the central government and the RBI. In practice, however, partnerships with a foreigner are almost non-existent.

Capital Structure

There is no minimum capital to be subscribed to in a partnership. The liability of a partner is not limited, and partners are jointly liable for partnership obligations.

Relationship of Partners

The rights and duties of the partners in a partnership are determined by an agreement among them and spelled out in the partnership agreement. Any matter not covered in the partnership agreement is determined by the Indian Partnership Act of 1932 or the Indian Contract Act of 1872.

Books and Records

There is no legal requirement to keep books and records relating to the accounts of the company's operations in any particular manner. However, proper books have to be maintained for income tax purposes.

Statutory Audit

Auditing partnership accounts is not required under the Partnership Act, but an audit under the Income Tax Act is compulsory if the turnover of the partnership exceeds a prescribed limit, presently Rs4 million for a business organisation.

Dissolution

A partnership may be dissolved with the consent of all the partners or in accordance with the provisions of the partnership agreement. Special circumstances may require compulsory dissolution of partnerships. For example, a partnership may be dissolved if it is declared insolvent. It may also be dissolved by the court if a partner files a suit. Subject to an agreement among the partners, the assets of the partnership are first used to pay off the debts of the firm. The partners are later given the profits.

Special Provisions for a Sole Proprietorship?

There are no special legal provisions that correspond to the Companies or Partnership Acts for a sole proprietorship. One exception is this—an audit under the Income Tax Act is compulsory if the turnover of a business organisation exceeds a prescribed limit of Rs4 million.

CHAPTER 6

Opening Up the Stock Market to Foreign Investment

On 12 April 1988, the Securities and Exchange Board of India (SEBI) was constituted as a non-statutory body, the result of a resolution passed by the government. The SEBI was to deal with all matters relating to the development and regulation of the securities market and investor protection. It was also to advise the government on the aforesaid matters.

An ordinance promulgated on 30 January 1992 gave the SEBI statutory status and powers. The ordinance provided for the establishment of a board to protect the interests of investors and to promote the development and regulation of the securities market. On 4 April 1992, the ordinance was replaced by an Act of Parliament. Under the act, the SEBI's main functions were to:

- Prohibit insider trading in securities
- Prohibit fraudulent and unfair trade practices relating to the securities market
- Regulate the business in stock exchanges and any other securities market
- Regulate substantial acquisition of shares and takeover of companies
- Register and regulate the operation of stockbrokers, sub-brokers, share transfer agents, bankers to an issue, trustees of trust deeds, registrars to an issue, merchant bankers, underwriters, portfolio managers and other intermediaries associated with the securities market
- Register and regulate the workings of collective investment schemes, including mutual funds

- Promote and regulate self-regulatory organisations
- Promote the education of investors and provide training for the intermediaries of the securities market

The SEBI inspected several stock exchanges in the period 1994 to 1995 and prepared inspection reports. The Ministry of Finance issued a notification on 13 September 1994 and delegated SEBI some powers by the Securities Contracts (Regulation) Act of 1956. This was done to strengthen the regulatory powers of the SEBI. As a result, the SEBI is now in a better position to effectively regulate the stock market.

Stock Exchanges

Stock exchanges are managed by their governing boards and executive directors. Overall, they are regulated by the Ministry of Finance and the SEBI.

The number of joint stock companies—government and non-government-owned—incorporated under the Companies Act of 1956 and operational in India as from 31 March 1994 is 308,324. Of these, 305,625 companies are limited by shares, 349 companies have unlimited liability and 2,350 are limited by guarantee or are non-profit associations. The 305,625 companies limited by shares have a paid-up capital of Rs104,890.8 crore. Out of these, there are 38,000 public limited companies and 267,625 private limited companies with a paid-up capital of Rs70,112.1 crore and Rs34,778.7 crore respectively.

Stock exchanges play an important role in mobilising financial resources for the corporate sector. They provide an organised market for transactions in shares and other securities. There are presently 22 stock exchanges in the country, which are recognised by the government under the Securities Contracts (Regulations) Act of 1956. The stock exchanges are located in Mumbai (two here), Calcutta, Chennai, New Delhi, Ahmedabad, Ludhiana, Kanpur, Jaipur, Indore, Pune, Hyderabad, Bangalore, Cochin,

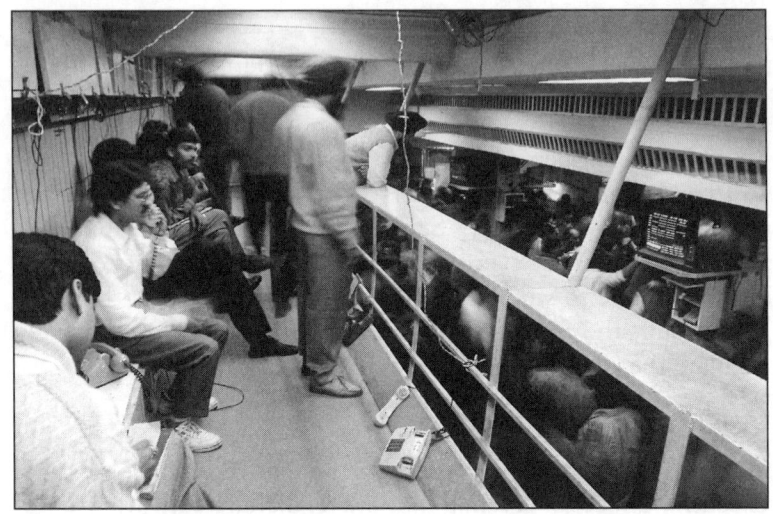

One of the many stock exchanges in India abuzz with activity.

Guwahati, Mangalore, Patna, Bhubaneshwar, Rajkot, Vadodara, Coimbatore and Meerut.

The registered office of the National Stock Exchange Limited (NSEL), which was granted recognition on 26 April 1993, is in Mumbai. The NSEL is expected to function as a model stock exchange with an automated screen-based system, which will provide services to investors across the country.

Out of the 23 stock exchanges, five were established after 1978. A few more are expected to come up in the near future. By July 1996, 9,000 companies were listed on the stock exchanges with a paid-up capital of Rs1,05,284 crore. Their market capitalisation was estimated at Rs5,26,476 crore. In 1985, the Bombay Stock Exchange alone accounted for 70% of the overall listed capital in the country and 80% of the overall market capitalisation. The workings of the Bombay Stock Exchange is widely believed to be reflective of what is happening in the rest of the stock exchanges in the country, barring two or three.

Volume of Transactions

The total turnover of transactions (a number of transactions goes unreported) in the period 1995 to 1996 was around Rs50,000 crore at the Bombay Stock Exchange. Out of this total volume of transactions, both forward or speculative transactions, where there is no intention to take or give deliveries of shares, and cost delivery shares are involved. The remaining transactions involve deliveries of shares. Only around 3% of the deliveries represent purchases or sales of securities by genuine investors, the rest arising from carry-forward transactions. The total market capitalisation of the Bombay Stock Exchange as at 31 July 1997 was Rs5573.07 billion.

Working Hours and Days

The working hours of the major stock exchanges in Mumbai, Calcutta, New Delhi, etc. are from 10 in the morning to half past three in the afternoon. They operate for approximately 150 to 200 days a year and are closed for trading on Saturdays, Sundays and public holidays.

Stockbrokers

There are around 7,500 stockbrokers in the country. A number of these active stockbrokers, especially the enterprising ones, have branched out to allied lines of business, such as merchant banking, portfolio management, financial and investment consultancy, and management of fixed deposits, public issues, etc. Some have created a small network of correspondents in important centres of the country. They use the latest technology to process applications, as well as research and analyse investment prospects.

Other such active stockbrokers are involved in underwriting new issues and publishing investment newsletters, magazines, etc. They establish close links with leading foreign merchant bankers, investment bankers and commercial banks in the developed world and, at the same time, develop contacts in the developing countries. These entrepreneurial stockbrokers swap information on

It is not all work and no play at the stock exchanges across India. After a hard day's work, stockbrokers celebrate a fellow colleague's birthday.

companies, industries, investment opportunities, probable collaborations, syndication of loans, etc. In the process, they get good exposure and gain the necessary experience from international dealings, as well as the technical know-how of such dealings. Unfortunately the number of such enterprising stockbrokers are still few and far between for a country the size of India.

The Emerging Scenario

The private sector will have to raise fresh resources of the minimum order of Rs60,000 crore from the capital market between now and the years 1999 and 2000, making an average of about Rs4,300 crore a year. Out of the estimated total resources, Rs36,000 crore may be raised through debentures or debt-related instruments. This may be quoted on the stock exchanges, with Rs24,000 crore raised mainly by way of equity capital.

Other significant changes:

- The government has announced its intention to improve the operation of the stock exchanges.
- The difference in investor psychology will be evident, as investment consciousness becomes more and more widespread.
- The Unit Trust of India has floated the India Funds to attract the savings of non-Indian residents and others for investment in the country.
- The RBI is now favourably inclined to permit well-established companies to issue money and market instruments like short-dated commercial paper, subject to certain conditions.
- The Unit Trust of India has floated several mutual funds schemes of master shares for the benefit of small shareholders in the country.
- The government is contemplating the possibility of relaxing the debt-equity ratios in a number of industries.
- The government is making serious attempts to improve the efficiency of public sector enterprises in order to enhance their profitability and reduce the drain on the National Exchequer.
- Nearly 65% of the existing shareholding population hail from only five centres in the case of 80 large companies. They are Mumbai, New Delhi, Calcutta, Ahmedabad and Chennai. Plans are underway to increase the number of centres.
- The primary market is more active and organised now than in the past. Expertise, organisational abilities and sophistication are built into marketing strategies.

The economic climate, thus, offers good prospects for the private sector to mobilise the required resources.

Predictions for the years 1999 and 2000 if changes are effected:

- The investor population may stand at 50 million.
- There may be at least 600 new issues every year.

- The number of stock issues of listed companies may total 10,000 to 12,000.
- The total volume of transactions may total Rs75,000 crore for all the stock exchanges of the country.
- The actual number of individual transactions increase to around 50 million.
- Assuming that 90% of the paid-up capital of all the public limited companies in the future continue to be listed on the stock exchanges, the stock exchanges may end up having an additional 7,000 to 7,500 companies listed with them. This makes a total of 12,000 to 12,500 listed companies with a paid-up capital of about Rs30,000 crore and market capitalisation of about Rs 90,000 crore.
- If only 10 million out of the 15 million investors require the services of stockbrokers by the years 1999 and 2000, each stockbroker will be able to service around 1,000 investors. On this assumption, the stock exchanges will require a total membership of at least 10,000 active stockbrokers with a wide network of sub-brokers and agents. The Bombay Stock Exchange may require around 2,500 active stockbrokers compared to the 300 stockbrokers presently employed.

FIIs registered with the SEBI are permitted to invest in the equity of listed Indian companies on an automatic approval basis within prescribed limits. The following changes have been made to the regulations in regard to investment by FIIs:

- The limit on investment by FIIs in the total issued capital of individual companies has been raised from 5% to 10%.
- FIIs are now allowed to invest in unlisted companies to the same extent as in listed companies.
- FIIs are now allowed to invest in Debt Securities up to 100% after obtaining the specific approval of the SEBI.

Euro-issues

Euro-issues or issues in the form of bonds by Indian corporations on the European market were not permitted in the past as they were regarded a contingent liability to the companies in foreign exchange. They were restricted to a select group of companies or were allowed only by special approval. After assessing the economic situation, the Ministry of Finance liberalised the guidelines for Euro-issues (guidelines were issued in 1993 and modified by the government in 1994). The salient features of the guidelines are summarised below:

- Companies procuring funds through Euro-issues are now permitted to remit funds into India in anticipation of the use of the funds or to preserve the funds as foreign currency deposits with banks and financial institutions.
- The ceiling for utilising proceeds from Euro-issues for general corporate restructuring, including working capital requirements has been revised from 15% to 25%.
- The requirement of a three-year track record of good performance has been relaxed for companies seeking to finance infrastructure projects through Euro-issues.
- Restrictions imposed previously on the number of issues that could be floated by an individual company or group of companies during a financial year have been removed.
- Banks, financial institutions and non-banking finance companies registered with the RBI are now permitted to raise funds through Euro-issues. Investing the funds in stock markets and real estate, however, are not allowed.

Exchange Control Regulations

The RBI has modified its earlier guidelines on the pricing of preferential issues of shares. It now has listed companies for non-residents in order to bring them in line with the guidelines issued by the SEBI. The guidelines stipulate that the minimum price be fixed at the higher of the average price of the shares in the six months or two weeks immediately preceding the date of issue. The earlier RBI guidelines had the minimum issue price fixed at the average price of the shares for the preceding six months.

The guidelines issued by the RBI on the disinvestment of listed equity shares by foreign investors have been revised. Henceforth, the RBI will grant permission on an automatic basis for transferring shares from non-residents to residents, provided the sale is made on a stock exchange at the prevailing market price through a registered merchant banker or stockbroker.

The RBI will also grant permission on an automatic basis for transferring shares through a private arrangement, where the transfer price is equal to the average quotation of the shares for the week immediately preceding the date of application (with a permissible variation of 5%). Where the disinvestment is by foreign promoters in favour of existing Indian promoters with the objective of transferring management control, the transfer price should not exceed the average quotation of the shares for the preceding week by more than 25%.

Non-resident Indians (NRIs), Overseas Corporate Bodies and FIIs have been given general permission to subscribe up to 24% (in aggregate) on a repatriable basis to new issues of shares and convertible debentures of Indian companies engaged in manufacturing activities, including finance, hire purchase, leasing, trading and other services, except agricultural and plantation activities.

External Commercial Borrowings

In April 1995, the outgoing government stated its policy and procedures for obtaining approval for External Commercial Borrowings (ECBs). The policy essentially provided that ECBs can be raised only for meeting the foreign exchange cost of capital investment and that the borrowings should have a minimum final maturity period of five years.

The Ministry of Finance revised the policy in regard to ECBs in June 1996. The main features of the new policy are summarised as follows:

- A minimum average maturity period of three years has been prescribed in respect of ECBs equal to or less than US$15 million equivalent. In respect of borrowings exceeding this limit, a minimum average maturity of seven years will apply.
- Corporations and institutions have been given permission to raise ECBs to US$3 million equivalent with a simple maturity of three years. Such proceeds can also be utilised for rupee expenditure provided only one such loan is outstanding at any one time.
- New infrastructure and greenfield projects have been given permission to avail ECBs up to 35% of the total project cost. In the case of power projects, greater flexibility will be exercised based on the merits of each case.
- Infrastructure projects in the power, telecommunications and railway sectors have been given permission to procure ECBs to fund project-related rupee expenditure. Telecommunications companies have been given permission to use ECBs for financing licence fee payments.
- Re-financing outstanding amounts under existing loans by raising fresh loans at lower costs will henceforth be permitted.

Securities Law

- The entry norms for companies accessing the capital market have been tightened. The SEBI states that in order to get its securities listed on any stock exchange, a company should have a track record of dividend payment of at least three out of the five years immediately preceding the first public offer for equity or convertible securities. However, the SEBI has clarified that companies with no such track record can access the capital market, provided their projects are appraised by a public financial institution or a scheduled commercial bank. Such an appraising entity is in part financing the project by way of a loan or equity participation to the extent of at least 5% of the project cost.

- The SEBI has provided that the track record of dividend payments for three years will not apply to banks if they wish to access the capital market. In addition, public sector banks can make a premium issue if they have a two-year track record of profitability compared to the three-year track record requirement for other companies.

- The SEBI has provided that existing listed companies proposing to access the capital market must satisfy either a three-year track record criteria or have their projects appraised by a public financial institution or bank with a loan or equity participation of at least 5% in the company. This must be done if their equity capital after any offer to the public for equity or any convertible security is more than five times the equity capital prior to the offer.

- The SEBI has removed all categories of preferential allotment, except those made to promoters and promoter groups from the mandatory lock-in period requirement. In addition, in the case of listed companies, which have a track record of dividend payment in at least three out of the preceding five years, there will be no lock-in or minimum contribution requirement on the promoter's subscription to a public issue.

- The SEBI stipulates that a minimum 50% of the net offer to the public be allocated to individual investors applying for securities, including shares (not exceeding 1,000 in each case). The remaining 50% of the public offer could be allocated to corporate bodies and individuals applying for more than 1,000 securities. In both categories, the allotment will continue to be made on the basis of the proportionate allocation.

- The SEBI has relaxed the minimum subscription requirement of 90% in each case involving offers for sale of existing shares to the public. However, this requirement has been retained for public rights issues of equity and convertible securities. The requirement of a minimum 90% subscription has also been relaxed in the case of exclusive debt issues, provided the issuer makes adequate disclosures about alternative sources of finance that have been tied up.

- The SEBI permits companies to list their debt securities on a stock exchange even if the equity of such companies is not listed.

- The SEBI permits companies issuing securities exceeding Rs1 billion to the public by way of a prospectus to utilise the book building facility. This facility can be utilised to the extent that a percentage of the issue is reserved for a firm allotment as per the existing SEBI guidelines.

In September 1995, the president of India promulgated the Depositories Ordinance, thereby paving the way for the establishment of depositories and the introduction of paperless trading in securities. The key provisions of the ordinance are as follows:

- Depositories will be established as companies registered with the SEBI.

- Depositories will appoint participants, that is, custodians, large brokerage houses, etc. Investors will have access to the depositories through these participants.

- Securities with depositories will be fungible.

- Investors will have the option to either hold the security or register with the depository.

- Depositories will be liable for loss caused by negligence.

Opportunities for Investment

The Giant Beckons

With the levelling off of economic growth in the developed world, the developing countries in Asia offer international firms and individual investors the best prospects for investment. Taiwan, Korea, Hong Kong and Japan, with the exception of the Philippines, have reached high levels of economic development, while the countries of Southeast Asia—Indonesia, Malaysia, Thailand, Singapore and Brunei, Myanmar (previously Burma)— are rapidly increasing their economic development levels. The economic crisis plaguing these countries now, however, has temporarily altered this view.

Other regions of the world, such as Africa, are still below the "threshold of attractiveness"; for reasons ranging from political strife to poor levels of economic development, investors hesitate to put their money into these countries.

As their optimal positions on the development curve suggest, the South Asian countries—Pakistan, Bangladesh, Sri Lanka, Maldives, Nepal, Bhutan and India—offer dramatic investment opportunities. The economies are poised to grow as a result of the various new policies introduced by the governments in the last few years. India, unaffected by the economic crisis that has taken its toll on many Southeast countries, offers the investor unique advantages.

About the People

Education and the Workforce

Education is compulsory at the primary level. However, the literacy rate on the average is below 55% for the nation as a whole,

Many companies conduct management training courses to upgrade the skills of their workers.

although some states like Kerala and West Bengal—both known for long periods of communist rule—have attained high literacy rates of above 90%. Bihar, the country's most economically backward state, has a literacy rate of below 30%.

The education system generally provides for the learning of three languages—English, Hindi (the national language) and a regional or state language. Education up to secondary school level may be conducted in any of the three languages. However, advanced education is invariably conducted in English.

On a comparative basis to other countries in Southeast Asia, one of the advantages India enjoys is a workforce highly educated in the technical and management fields. The pool has grown from 100,000 to around 5 million people now. However, the industrial sector has not come forward to invest large sums of money in research as the gestation period is fairly long and the returns uncertain. This is despite the fact that the government gives tax breaks to those industrial firms that carry out research. Another advantage India enjoys is that English is a tool of communication in business. Communication, thus, presents no major problem to foreigners.

West Bengal: A State Transformed

In 1994, the state government of West Bengal undertook a new industrial policy that welcomed foreign investment on mutually advantageous terms. Within a year, the state saw over 70 new projects at different stages of implementation. West Bengal now ranks second in the country with regard to foreign direct investment. Investors will be pleased to know that the state's labour force is skilled, organised and registers high productivity.

Population Distribution

In India, the average number of persons per household is five. The ratio of females per 1,000 males is 927:1,000 (1991 census). The urban-rural divide is around 300 million urban and 630 million rural. With an annual population growth rate of 1.8%, India has a sizeable population in the 15 to 59 age group, unlike countries in the West and Japan, which have a higher ageing population. This is an important indicator for market surveyors and corporate planners as it shows the likely trend in consumer tastes.

Upper and Middle Class Markets

When the Indian economy opened up, many foreign companies set up shop in India. As a consequence, international brands ranging from clothes and cosmetics to cars and electronics are now available in India. On the Linking Road in Bandra, a prosperous Mumbai suburb, the street is lined with foreign brand stores, such as Levi's, DKNY, Benetton, Baskin & Robbins and McDonald's. The nation's rapidly growing middle class cannot seem to get enough of these products.

Distribution of Population by Age (1991)

Population (Mn)			Percentage Distribution		
Age Group (years)	Male	Female	Total	Male	Female	Total
0–4	57.5	52.9	110.9	13.1	13.0	13.1
5–14	102.8	93.2	196.3	23.4	22.9	23.2
15–19	49.2	42.3	91.4	11.2	10.4	0.8
20–24	41.3	39.5	81.2	9.4	9.7	9.6
25–34	66.3	62.3	128.6	15.1	15.3	15.2
35–44	48.8	45.6	93.9	11.1	11.2	11.1
45–54	35.1	33.0	68.6	8.0	8.1	8.1
55–59	13.6	12.6	26.2	3.1	3.1	3.1
60 & above	25.0	25.6	50.8	5.7	6.3	6.0
Total	439.2	407.1	846.3	100.0	100.0	100.0

Note: Data excludes Jammu and Kashmir. Percentage Distribution is based on the estimate prepared by the Registrar General of India, while figures under Population are derived. Due to rounding off, the sums of the constituent data under various age groups may not tally with the total.

Source: Statistical Outline of India, 1996–1997

In the high income bracket, there are around 50 million people in India who can compete with people in the developed countries of the West in terms of their net worth irrespective of whether this is reflected in the taxes they pay. With the sugar barons of Maharashtra and a middle class of another 200 to 300 million people spread throughout the major and minor cities of India and in some pockets of advanced agricultural areas, such as the Punjab and Haryana in the north, India has an attractive and growing market for almost all varieties of goods and services.

One effect of a liberalised economy is that people now have more disposable income. More are buying such things as imported cars, cellular phones, pagers and branded jeans.

Entrepreneurial Class

India has a strong entrepreneurial class of people who seize every opportunity to become successful in business. Entrepreneurship tends to be strongest in the states of Gujarat, Rajasthan, Andhra Pradesh and Maharashtra, least in the central and northern Indian states of Bihar, Uttar Pradesh, Madhya Pradesh, Himachal Pradesh and Kashmir, and moderate in the coastal states of Kerala, Tamil Nadu, Orissa and West Bengal. This is on account of various ethnic and historical factors. Indians living on the western coast of the country like Gujarat have had greater exposure to international trade and visitors; hence, people there have turned out to be more business oriented.

Employment and Income

Progress in the employment sector has been mixed. While registered job seekers have increased to 36 million, there is large-scale under-employment as far as agricultural workers and owners of small holdings are concerned. The reason is because these workers are employed only seasonally in the rural areas. However, unemployment is prevalent even in the cities such that it is not uncommon for the highly qualified to take on menial jobs.

Employment			
	Organised sector employment	Registered job seekers	Man days lost
1950–1951	N.A.	0.3	12.8
1960–1961	12.1	1.8	6.5
1970–1971	17.5	5.1	20.6
1980–1981	22.9	17.8	21.9
1990–1991	26.7	34.6	24.1
1993–1994	27.4	36.3	20.3
1994–1995	N.A.	36.7	21.0
1995–1996	N.A.	36.8	11.3

Source: Statistical Outline of India, 1996–1997

The table that follows shows India's national income, per capita income and population figures from 1950 to 1996. Despite all-time highs in absolute income figures in the period 1995 to 1996, Indians are not necessarily better off now. A hundredfold increase in national income since the 1950s has been offset by the tripling of the population and inflation rates of between 7%–8% and 12%–13% per annum. Purchasing power has dwindled because rising costs of living have eclipsed increments in per capita incomes.

India's per capita income of Rs9,350 is around USD300. The purchasing power parity developed by the World Bank is below USD1,300.

Income and Population Growth

	National Income (in US millions)	Per Capita Income (Rupee)	Population (Mn)
1950–1951	214.4	249	239
1960–1961	356.1	350	328
1970–1971	912.6	729	675
1980–1981	2767.1	1,808	1,630
1990–1991	10,451.9	5,605	4,983
1991–1992	11,990.3	6,340	5,603
1992–1993	13,650.6	7,098	6,262
1993–1994	15,949.9	8,103	7,185
1994–1995	18,716.3	9,328	8,282
1995–1996	21,439.3	10,519	9,312
1996–1997	24,333.6	11,735	10,399

Source: Statistical Outline of India, 1997–1998

Laying the Foundations: Infrastructure

While an understanding of the existing infrastructure is important for the business person, he or she must note the more crucial fact that an expansion of and improvement to the existing infrastructure presents good opportunities for investment.

Roads

Most of India's infrastructure, especially the road system, has been in an appalling condition until quite recently. The state of the roads is expected to improve with privatisation, which is a relatively recent development in India.

The roads in India on a normal working day. The present road network is a potential investment area. Improvements to it will increase the country's economic competitiveness.

Railways

More could be done to improve India's railways, the most effective form of public transport in the country.

The government has initiated a scheme for private sector participation in the railway sector under the Build, Own, Lease and Transfer scheme (BOLT). The government has also identified the following projects for which private participation may be invited under BOLT:

- Gauge conversion
- Rolling stock projects
- Doublings
- Round over-bridges
- Bridges
- Electrification
- Telecommunications

The Railway Board also plans to streamline policies to help private companies own and operate wagons.

Power

There continues to be a shortage of power, particularly for industrial use. To keep pace with the high demand and huge consumption of power, the government has allowed the private sector to set up barge-mounted power plants and diesel engine generating units using heavy fuel oils (except high-speed diesel). It has also formulated a broad policy in regard to the setting up of mega projects (i.e. power projects with the capacity of generating 1,000 megawatts and above of power that can be supplied to more than one state).

Central Electricity Authority (CEA) clearance is now required for power projects with a project cost exceeding Rs4 billion (Rs1 billion previously). This will be awarded under a competitive bidding procedure. CEA approval is required for all other projects where the project cost exceeds Rs1 billion.

Captive and co-generation power plants are exempt from obtaining CEA approval. However, approval of the State Electricity Board (SEB) will remain a requirement. The SEB will refer the proposal to the CEA if the capacity of such power plants exceeds 25 megawatts.

The government has formulated guidelines in regard to the renovation and modernisation of thermal plants, and the renovation, modernisation and upgrading of hydro power plants.

Ports

India needs to shore up its ports. The waiting time for ships at Mumbai's harbour, for example, often exceeds 30 days. The government is presently liberalising the construction and management of smaller ports along India's large coastline, as well as seeking foreign help in expanding its principal ports.

In order to meet its targets of expansion and modernisation of ports, the government has sought the participation of the private sector. While the process of private sector participation in the major ports is still under the purview of the central government, the state governments have been given the autonomy to come up with policies encouraging their participation with respect to the minor and intermediate ports.

The government has called for private sector participation in:

- Dredging
- Leasing port facilities
- Establishing container terminals
- Establishing warehousing and storage facilities
- Operating and maintaining cargo handling terminals
- Providing pilotage and cranage services
- Maintaining port craft and other equipment

Water

The availability and utilisation of water is sub-optimal, with cities often running short of this basic necessity. In the agricultural sector, the poor irrigation system results in a great deal of water shortage and wastage. The supply of drinking water to villages is also inadequate.

India's agriculture is dependent on the monsoons. By the end of 1996, irrigation support was available to 89.42 million hectares of land under cultivation. However, while the monsoons result in a good supply of rain seasonally, this potential water source has not been adequately harnessed. What is more, dam projects for improving the irrigation system often run into ecological and human resettlement difficulties.

Agriculture and Processed Food

Over 70% of the population depends directly or indirectly on agriculture. The principal crops in India are rice, wheat, cotton, groundnuts, grapes, mustard, sesame seeds, linseed, sugarcane, jute, castor seeds, tea, coffee and rubber. Food crops dominate agricultural production in India and cover about 81% of the total area under cultivation. Non-food crops cover the remaining sown area.

Presently, agricultural productivity registers high growth levels. Although the area of land under cultivation has shown no marked change over the last 20 years, the total agricultural yield has increased from 85.3 million tonnes in 1974 to 148.2 million tonnes in 1994 (Source: India Development Report (1997) on Index of Agricultural Input).

The Indian government has liberalised the food-processing industry. While large holdings by private corporations are not permitted owing to the various land ceiling acts, the government now encourages cooperative contribution by small land-holders. The reason is to facilitate optimisation by enabling private firms and cooperatives to process foods for the purpose of value addition.

Any growth in the infrastructure sector translates into an enormous potential for growth in the agriculture sector and others. This, coupled with a few more reforms to the sector, will see the food and agriculture sector registering one of the biggest growths among the different sectors.

Conquering the Skies

Air traffic has been liberalised: private operators are now permitted. The competition has improved the service and punctuality of the state-owned Indian Airlines. However, controversy surrounds the Singapore Airlines-Tata venture, which was not cleared by the Indian government. The Tatas then decided to go ahead with the project themselves and obtained approval from the Foreign Investment Promotion Board. However, they failed to obtain clearance at the cabinet committee level.

The latest policy changes (Budget 1998) on airlines stipulates some new requirements. The main one is that any joint venture for setting up an airline cannot be formed with a foreign airlines or an investing firm with airline links or investments. This has been done to ensure that a strong international airline does not have a back door entry into India through a local investor, thereby "killing off" the domestic airlines industry. The Tata venture for an airline now has tie-ups with foreign institutions and other investors.

India is well-connected by air to major cities around the world. Major international airports are located in Mumbai and New Delhi. Other international airports are located in Calcutta, Chennai, Bangalore, Trivandrum and Goa. Many new international airports are needed to speed up the economic development of the country as well as increase the number of tourist arrivals to different parts of the country.

Tourism

India abounds with places of tourist interest and probably offers a greater diversity for tourists (in terms of places to see) than any

Tourists have a taste of Indian food in a popular Indian restaurant.

other country in the world. The tourism sector, thus far underexploited, provides a good area for investment. The main reasons for the underexploitation are:

- Lack of proper infrastructure, such as good air connections (domestically), roads and hotels, which are available only in major tourist areas
- Negative perception in the minds of tourists that India is a place of poverty, squalor, disease, risk and inconvenience. These descriptive labels are often exaggerations of the real situation.

Foreign business persons can explore the investment opportunities in the tourism sector as such factors as cost of land, geographical landscape and climate are to their advantage.

A Government Priority

Developing the tourism sector is a major priority for the Indian government. Towards this end, hotels will be expanded and the capacity of airlines increased. Five international and 14 domestic airports will be expanded and modernised. A survey by the Federation of Industry and Commerce indicates that over the next two to three years, an investment of $12 million is needed for the tourism sector to meet its goals. One-third of the investment is expected to come from the government and the rest from private investment.

Telecommunications

The telecommunications sector has improved dramatically in the last few years. There is, for instance, a greater frequency of e-mail connections in India than in some developed countries. With telecommunications becoming a major growth area, Siemens, CIT-Alcatel and Fujitsu, among others, have set up production facilities in India.

The Union Cabinet has approved an ordinance for setting up the Telecom Regulatory Authority of India (TRAI), a watchdog authority for the telecommunications sector. The TRAI will deal with post-licence issues, such as tariffs, inter-operator problems, operating standards and customer services.

The main functions of the TRAI include:

- Ensuring technical compatibility and effective inter-relationship between different service providers

- Regulating arrangements among service providers so they share the revenue derived from providing telecommunications services
- Ensuring all service providers comply with the licence conditions
- Laying down and ensuring the time period for providing local and long distance circuits of telecommunications between different service providers
- Settling disputes between service providers
- Protecting the interests of consumers using telecommunications services

---

Cellular Telephones: Growth Anticipated
In cities like Mumbai, New Delhi, Calcutta and Chennai, there are many mobile-phone service providers. The services are usually run by an Indian company in joint venture with a foreign company. Some of the foreign companies involved are France Telecom, Telstra of Australia and Telecom Malaysia. Ericsson's Almof predicts that cellular subscribers in India will grow from zero to around 3 million by the year 2005.

Insurance

Dominated by the public sector, insurance has been closed to the private sector and foreign investment. This remains a major controversy, with pressure not to privatise coming from lobbies within the insurance sector. In the 1998 budget speech, Yashwant Sinhe, finance minister of India, announced that the insurance sector would soon be opened to the private sector. It would, however, initially be restricted to only Indian players, that is, it will not be opened to foreign companies for now.

As part of its commitment to the privatisation programme, the government intends to go ahead with liberalising the insurance sector. Both foreign and Indian companies will be allowed to enter the industry. The government is recodifying the existing legislation governing the insurance sector. Based on the recommendations of the Malhotra Committee, which prepared an agenda of reforms for the Indian insurance sector, the government has set up an interim Insurance Regulatory Authority (IRA). The IRA is expected to function as a statutory body, regulating the insurance industry and granting approval to companies to enter the sector.

Electronics and Software

Electronics

Special incentives and infrastructural facilities have been developed to further boost the Indian electronics industry. The Rs 105 billion industry has achieved and maintained remarkable rates of growth. The annual growth rate accelerated to 35 % in the period 1985–1990 and 40% in 1997. Although the boom was essentially caused by a surge in the demand for consumer goods, the industry's product range now covers the entire gamut of electronics, from avionics, computer software and hardware to medical electronics and telecommunications equipment.

With the emphasis on technological upgrading, the government, national laboratories and private electronics industry are now channelling their energies into forging a strategic alliances.

Software

India's software development industry has already gained international recognition for its technical sophistication. The industry has progressed beyond the development of management information systems to the introduction of decision support systems in the manufacturing, telecommunications and service sectors. The software industry has also developed expertise in conversion methodologies and operations in the latest technological environment.

Crucial to the industry's phenomenal growth is the existence of a large, highly educated technical workforce. Recognising this particular asset, major international companies, such as IBM, have located new regional software development centres in India. Microsoft is also investing in a major way in India. Other major electronics companies now located in the country and growing rapidly include Motorola, Texas Instruments, Digital, Hewlett-Packard, Unisys, Siemens Nixdorf and Groupe Bull. Modern industry has also fuelled the demand for electronic process control and instrumentation, resulting in the operational expansion of Honeywell, Taylor and Bosch in India.

Bangalore

Software development is now a billion-dollar industry in India, and Bangalore, dubbed the "Silicon Valley of India", is where most of the action is. The city, one of India's most liberal and cosmopolitan, has a good mix of domestic and foreign computer firms and enjoys a healthy annual growth rate. There are around 300 software companies in the city, although most of them are owned by Indians. Foreign companies like Motorola, Texas Instruments, Sun Microsystems and others account for some 70% of Bangalore's new investment.

Bangalore is an ideal place for investment due to its location and large pool of highly educated young people. These people, many of whom are employed in the software industry, have given the city a noticeable "yuppie" culture. The city also has several cyber-cafés, where people can surf the Internet with a cup of coffee in their hands.

Technology Parks

The electronics sector received a further boost in 1996 through a policy that encourages the setting up of Electronic Hardware Technology Parks (EHTPs) and Software Technology Parks (STPs). These parks are intended not only to build a strong, efficient and competent electronics industry but also to enhance the export potential of the sector. Like Export Processing Zones (EPZs), the parks are exempt from duties.

Export Processing Units: A Closer Look

EPZs are an effective means of boosting the exports of a country. This has been especially so in a developing country like India. The zones, set up as enclaves and separated from the domestic tariff area by physical barriers, are intended to provide a low-cost, duty-free environment for competitive export production.

India has seven EPZs in Kandla (Gujarat), Santacruz (Maharashtra), Cochin (Kerala), Chennai (Tamil Nadu), NOIDA (within the National Capital Region in Uttar Pradesh), Falta (West Bengal) and Vishakhapatnam (Andhra Pradesh). In these zones, the government provides basic infrastructural facilities like developed plots for the construction of factory buildings, sheds, roads, power and water supply, drainage, customs clearance facilities, banks and post offices. The facilities are available in a service centre located within each zone.

Seven Software/Hardware Technology Development Parks have been set up in Bangalore, Bhubaneshwar, Gandhinagar, Hyderabad, NOIDA, Pune and Trivandrum. Both STPs and EHTPs are 100% export-oriented projects for developing software/electronics hardware technologies.

The objectives of STPs and EHTPs are to:

- Provide training for professionals in software technology
- Develop infrastructural resources, such as communication facilities, core computers, buildings, amenities, etc.
- Undertake and encourage design and development in the field of computer software and software engineering

The new policy gives entrepreneurs greater flexibility in commercial decisions. Value addition (defined as the net foreign exchange earned by the unit expressed as a percentage of the FOB value of exports) and access to the domestic market are not defined in any rigid manner but are combined together. Entrepreneurs are free to select the combination that best suits their requirements.

Incentives for Investment

A 100% direct foreign equity is permissible in EHTP and STP units. EHTP units may combine both computer hardware and software operations, with the requirement that the minimum value addition for software be 60% and the DTA (Domestic Tariff Area) sale of software be limited to 25% of the production of software in value terms. As a special incentive, the income generated by software exports qualifies for 100% tax deduction. The address and contact number for enquiries and applications is:

The Joint Secretary,
Department of Electronics,
Electronics Niketan,
6, CGO Complex, New Delhi–110 003
Tel: 91–11–4363093
Fax: 91–11–4363134 and 4363083

In order to encourage exports, the Indian government provides special incentives to units set up primarily for manufacturing goods for export. Such units may be set up in EPZs or may be 100% Export Oriented Units (EOUs) outside EPZs.

EOUs were introduced in early 1981 to complement the EPZs. EOUs are similar to EPZs but located outside the EPZs, where infrastructure needs are greater. EOUs offer a wider source of raw materials, ports to facilitate exports, hinterland facilities and technological skills. In addition, they offer an industrial base and a larger land area for projects. The workings of the EOU are reviewed from time to time through interaction with business people and entrepreneurs who have set up units in these zones to resolve problems within individual units and make further improvements when required.

Incentives for EOU and EPZ units are as follows:

- EOU/EPZ units can import industrial input free of customs duties.
- A 100% foreign equity is welcomed in EOU/EPZ units.
- EOU/EPZ units can raise foreign currency loans, subject to certain conditions.
- Those with EOU/EPZ units are entitled to a tax holiday. They are exempt from payment of corporate income tax for a block period of five years in the first eight years of operation. Export earnings continue to be exempt from tax even after the tax holiday is over.
- Industrial plots and standard design factories are available to EOU/EPZ units at concessionary rates.
- FOB value of exports of EOU/EPZ units are added together to match those of parent/associate companies located in the domestic tariff area for the purpose of getting star trading house, trading house and export house status.
- Those with EOU/EPZ units are exempt from payment of central and state sales tax.
- Supplies from the DTA to EOU/EPZ units are deemed exports; hence, they do not qualify for payment of excise duties. This means that high-quality input is available at lower costs.
- EOU/EPZ units may export goods through star trading houses, trading houses and export houses.

By the NIP of 1991, most industries, except for a specified list, do not require an industrial licence.

Foreign Investment in EOU/EPZ Units

The government encourages foreign investment in EOU/EPZ units and freely permits up to 100% foreign equity in such units. Imported capital goods can be financed through foreign equity of up to Rs100 million. The product manufactured need not be licensed and is not reserved for the public sector. Automatic approval is available to proposals satisfying the following criteria:

- Foreign technology agreement, if any, entered into by the unit is restricted to a lump sum payment of Rs10 million or 8% royalty (net of taxes) over a period of five years from the start of production.
- The project attempts to achieve value addition of at least 20% unless otherwise specified.
- The project is located: (a) within an EPZ and availability of space and conformity with environmental and other standards of the EPZ have been certified by the Development Commissioner or (b) in an area other than an EPZ for which it complies with the conditions in regard to location required by the Department of Industrial Development.
- The unit meets the requirements of the customs authorities; the provisions of the Central Excise and Salt Act of 1944; and bonding by the customs. All manufacturing operations are carried out in the same premises (the proposal does not envisage sending out of the bonded area any raw materials or intermediate products for any other manufacturing or processing activity).
- The conditions relating to DTA sales are adhered to.
- The unit has an annual turnover of at least Rs500 million if it is for the manufacture of gems and jewellery, and the project is located outside EPZs and other designated areas.

Eligibility for 100% EOU/EPZ units

Units undertaking to export the entire production of goods may be set up under the EOU or EPZ schemes. Such units may be engaged in the manufacture of software, agriculture, aquaculture, animal husbandry, floriculture, horticulture, pisciculture, poultry and sericulture. Units engaged in service activities may also be considered on merit.

The Electronics Industry: A Final Look

Much of India's recent industrial growth and economic potential can be attributed to the liberalisation drive that began in 1991. Licensing formalities have been done away with, except in the case of some consumer and strategic electronics, but even here, the procedures have been considerably simplified.

Data communication needs for software technology parks are provided either through Packet Switch Data Network (PSDN) or dedicated earth stations. In collaboration with the French government, a new network has been established in New Delhi, Mumbai and Bangalore to facilitate highspeed data communication and computer connections between Indian companies and their overseas partners in Western Europe.

India's overall industrial goal, therefore, is to create an environment of high volume production boasting international quality and competitive cost structures. The 1997 prediction for the electronics industry was a turnover in excess of Rs360 billion.

International Arbitration

The opening up of India's economy and its fulfilment of requirements under the WTO agreement brought about an Arbitration and Conciliation Ordinance in 1996. The ordinance aims to consolidate and amend, among others, the laws relating to domestic arbitration, international commercial arbitration and the enforcement of foreign arbitral awards. The ordinance also defines the law relating to conciliation. The main provisions are as follows:

- The arbitrator now has the power to determine the venue of arbitration and the power to choose the law applicable to the arbitration proceedings (both procedural and substantive) if the parties involved fail to reach any agreement.
- Any intervention by the courts is permitted only on some fundamental grounds, such as the validity of the arbitration agreement and the violation of the principles of natural justice.
- The award will be enforceable in the same manner as if it were a final decree of the courts. No further confirmation from the courts is necessary.
- A similar procedure for enforcing foreign awards has been stipulated. An award is considered a foreign award if either of the two conventions—the Geneva Convention of 1927 or the New York Convention of 1958—apply, and the arbitration is held at a venue notified by the government for that purpose.
- The ordinance contains detailed provisions for conciliation. A distinctive feature of conciliation is that it demands the consensus of all the parties involved at every stage. The conciliator's role is to induce the parties to arrive at a settlement.

CHAPTER 8

Setting Up a Successful Joint Venture in India

Setting up a joint venture in a developing country, especially in a socially and politically complex country like India, is a potential minefield. While investment opportunities abound in the country, potential investors need to analyse the situation carefully, taking into account their goals and needs, before taking the plunge.

The Right Location

Before a company locates its business in India, it has to consider several factors like the availability of good infrastructure, incentives offered by the state government and the taxation rate. Many state governments now offer incentives in the form of tax holidays, land at lower prices and so on to attract foreign investment.

For a project to take off in any state, approval is required from both the state and central governments. Jurisdiction falls into three areas. The first area is a list of items controlled by the central government and generally covers such domains as national security, defence and foreign affairs. The second is the corporate area and covers such domains as excise, income tax and customs duties. The state governments have responsibility over local taxation, local law enforcement and the activities of the municipality, etc. In the third area, both the central and state governments have jurisdiction over such domains as labour law and legislation, price control, etc.

The central government has now begun streamlining the bureaucratic process in order to keep pace with the changes in legislation and opening up of the economy. However, in the local government bodies of some states, particularly in the municipalities, the streamlining process is not on par with that of the central government's.

A Suitable Partner

Foreign companies often look for joint venture partners on the basis of size without paying careful attention to the match between philosophy and business values. Many large family-owned Indian companies are not willing to change and choose to continue with a philosophy that tends to be more people-oriented than task-oriented. They have a hierarchical style of management and do not subscribe to the policy of "hire and fire". Foreign companies must, thus, choose their Indian partners wisely, preferably those who have built up relationships on a long-term basis.

Keep Your Eyes Peeled

It is important to keep in mind that a company that has served as an agent or a representative may not necessarily be the best choice for a partner in a joint venture. Some of these agents or representatives, despite their stints as "middlemen" in export-import transactions, do not have the necessary experience or resources to fulfil their responsibilities as joint venture partners.

Generally, Indian companies lack the experience to effectively market sophisticated products. Many major players of quality brands find that their Indian partners are not used to dealing with a different level or league of products and are unable to understand the nuances and differences between doing business in a globally competitive environment and a protected one. The result: foreign companies either opt to set up subsidiaries in India or attempt to take over the existing business.

Avoiding Shortcuts and Making Connections Work

While it is easy to say that business is often done on a handshake, this is only a commitment of spirit. Letters and specifics must be understood carefully and contractually agreed to. Many companies run into difficulties because they make compromises on account of embarrassment to put forth their conditions at the contractual level. Also, some find the details in the legal contract tedious and do not take the time to understand them. Such short cuts must be avoided.

It is important that a foreign investor builds his own base of local connections for a smooth running of both his business and personal life. The right connections with the bureaucracy, politicians, police, etc. may come in handy at a later time. It is to your advantage to be in the good books of all political parties, especially when setting up big projects.

Other Useful Notes for Investors

- Environmental clearances can be held up both at the central and state levels. Check with the Ministry of the Environment.
- For power connections, permission must first be sought from the local governments. These, at times, are slow in coming. Many states in India experience power shortage. For instance, investors who flocked to the southern Indian state of Karnataka and the popular investment centre of Bangalore have now been forced to create their own power generation facilities. However, even after creating their own facilities, they cannot sell the surplus power generated to adjacent plants without prior approval. This is because of the complex pricing structure of the power sector and the government's policy of distribution and investment. Nonetheless, investors need not worry unduly as these areas are getting adequate attention from the government. Also, many states in India now offer industrial estates with guaranteed power and water supply.

- Labour laws fall under the jurisdiction of both the central and state governments. Careful consideration must be paid to this when acquiring a firm with a large labour force. This is because the government has not yet come up with a clear-cut policy for retrenching surplus labour in firms acquired by new investors, be they Indians or foreigners.

- Allocation of land, water and some natural resources is done by the local government, and permission must be sought to use them. The process of obtaining approval and the implementation of regulatory requirements, such as the requirement of maintaining registers and the documentation of excise payments are complex, and entail inspections. A new firm in a joint venture must, therefore, understand the importance of making provisions for time and understanding of the long and tedious process of paper work in terms of the number of forms filled up, number of persons contacted and number of approvals obtained. It is recommended

Getting partners who understand your goals and needs is important. Always keep the communication channels open.

that a local individual who understands these issues be put in charge of the process so that he can "facilitate the process". At times, however, local agents may not be suitably qualified, so be sure of their credentials before hiring them.

• Economic studies show that many companies are obsessed with the idea of cost control when it comes to locating a business in a country. However, this consideration is often secondary to the accessibility of the market. The investor has to study the demography, as well as the income distribution and buying behaviour of the people carefully before deciding on the location. This is particularly important in a country like India where the transportation infrastructure has not yet been adequately developed. Most states are slow in undertaking infrastructural development projects because they face severe budgetary constraints. Important infrastructure constraints a foreign investor should consider are those relating to power, roads, airports, telecommunications, ports and water supply, among others.

Success Stories

Many investors and foreign companies have fortunately found the right partners, and instances of emerging joint ventures abound. Success is guaranteed if foreign investors enter the Indian market cautiously, and choose their local partners in a like manner. GE (General Electric), for instance, has done reasonably well in its venture with Indian appliance maker, Godrej. The tie-up benefited both companies: Godrej tapped into GE's technology to upgrade its appliances, while GE rode on Godrej's good reputation and distribution system.

Traditionally, tie-ups with big industrial groups have been the best bet for foreign investors. Several groups, such as the Tatas, Birlas, Goenkas and a few new ones, such as Reliance, are looked upon favourably for a joint venture since they dominate the market and have good connections. In fact, Reliance, the UB Group, the Tatas, Birlas, Modis, Mafatlals, Arvind Mills, Goenkas, Ranbaxy,

Lupin, Wockhardt and many other Indian companies, armed with a global mindset, have successful joint ventures in India and abroad. The Tata Group, for instance, has a joint venture with AT&T. The latter has dealings in the telecommunications sector with the Tata Group's rival, the Birlas.

That Tata Group also has a joint venture for power supply and environmental control systems with Liebert Corporation, a fairly large company based in the United States. The Tata Group brings its name and local connections to the venture, while Liebert Corporation brings with it technical know-how.

The List Goes On

Before the US$1.7 billion Duracell Corporation decided on a joint venture with the Poddar Group in India, it had discussions with Gillette, which was involved in an ongoing joint venture with Poddar. "Gillette shared a lot of information with us because they have a similar distribution pattern and we are non-competing," so said the vice-president of manufacturing for international development at Duracell. Eventually, Gillette introduced Duracell to the Poddar Group. A joint venture was born.

Usha India and Samsung Corporation have set up a manufacturing facility to produce transistors; Larsen & Toubro and Chiyoda have entered into a joint venture for carrying out extended engineering projects in India and abroad; Herberts and Jenson & Nicholson, a Swedish multinational company, has expressed interest in manufacturing automotive refinish paints in India; Renault has decided to join hands with Indonesia's Polysindo & Texmaco to establish a greenfield project in South India; and Dabur India and Antonio Puig have entered into a joint venture to set up manufacturing facilities in India and Nepal.

Fiat and Premier Automobiles entered into a joint venture to set up the Palio car project; Microsoft and ACI have entered into a joint venture to distribute computer software and hardware products; Toyota and Kirloskar have agreed to join hands to produce family type multipurpose vehicles; and HCL (Hindustan Computers Limited) and Cisco Systems intend to set up a software development centre in the technology park in Bangalore.

Omega's Foray into India

In the wake of the lifting of the government ban in 1996 on watches that cost more than 1,000 Swiss francs, a Singapore company is leading Omega (one of the oldest Swiss watch brands) on its passage to India. Formed in 1995, SMH S.E.A. is a joint venture between Singapore's luxury retailer BP de Silva Holdings and the world's largest watch manufacturer, SMH Holdings from Switzerland. However, with an import tax rate fixed at 90%, Omega has had to cut down on its prices in India to keep them similar to those in the rest of the world. Ravi Thakran, SMH S.E.A.'s manager for South and Southeast Asia, intends to double the Omega points of sale from the current 22 to 40 by tying up with all the leading watch and jewellery shops in important cities like Mumbai, Calcutta, Chennai and Hyderabad.

You Win Some, You Lose Some

Indian firms are sometimes at a disadvantage because of the financial strength of multinational companies. For instance, to maintain its earlier 34% holding, DCM would have had to provide Rs200 crore as its contribution to the issue of expanded capital, an amount it was unable to raise. DCM decided that a better strategy would be to sell some of its shares rather than passively renounce the rights, as this would bring no monetary gains but still result in a dilution of its holding.

Another case in point: the partnership between Tata Electric Locomotive Company (TELCO) and Mercedes-Benz. When Mercedes-Benz proposed further investment possibilities to expand the new product range and to set up a new chain of outlets for marketing their newly launched Mercedes-Benz cars in India, the Tatas could not take them up on their offer due to insufficient funds. The Tatas preferred instead to divest in favour of their partners.

Procter & Gamble and Godrej, who had a partnership in toiletry products, have gone their separate ways. Industry observers believe that the joint venture did not succeed because the result-oriented American firm wanted to make radical changes to the manpower, organisational structure and methods of marketing practised by Godrej.

It is also sometimes difficult to dislodge established Indian tastes and brands. Coca Cola, for example, bought an established Indian company Thums Up and tried to use its distribution system to dominate the soda market. Thums Up, however, still maintains its number one spot in India.

If Indian companies want to gain from their joint ventures with foreign firms, they must bargain from a position of strength. A study undertaken by CII (Confederation of Indian Industries) in collaboration with Rotary International revealed that some Indian firms entered into partnerships without any sharp perception of the market, made little value addition after a point, were afraid to sell out when it became necessary and therefore lost the trust of their foreign counterparts after a while.

The Case of Cargill Corporation

Cargill Corporation wanted to set up a salt processing unit in Gujarat. Although the state government approved the US$15 million foreign-owned firm with the commitment to export one million tonnes of salt, it later did not give the land to the multinational company. This was because of protests by the local small-scale firms who feared running out of business. That this could happen in the highly proactive Gujarat government surprised many. Foreign investors must, therefore, be prepared for the worst case scenario when they plan their investment strategy in India. Fortunately, this is not always the case.

An international company, which initially prefers to work with an Indian partner because of scarcity of human resources and prime office space, limited access to distribution channels, high cost entailed in setting up greenfield ventures on its own and lack of political contacts, quickly perceives the Indian partner's contribution as minimal. Once it gains a foothold in the Indian market, it often tries to shake off the Indian partner, who by then is looked upon as a liability rather than as an asset.

Since the general consensus is that FDI is necessary, a major concern now relates to the creation of the so-called level playing field. One way of interpreting this is to insist on applying all the rules and regulations of business in a uniform way. The argument is that the financial power of foreign firms must be neutralized, so domestic firms can compete with them on equal footing. Yet another area of concern is the attempts made by foreign companies to take over Indian companies; hence, the need for limits to foreign equity holdings.

Allowing 100% Subsidiaries

P.C. Chidambaram, former finance minister of India, felt that different rates of foreign equity holding were appropriate in different sectors. In 1994, the government headed by Narasimha Rao, former prime minister of India, announced that foreign investments by MNCs through joint ventures with Indian partners would take priority over the establishment of wholly-owned holding companies or subsidiaries. However, the government has been flexible and has permitted a number of MNCs to set up 100% subsidiaries and holding companies.

FIPB sources contend that 100% subsidiaries are allowed in some cases but not in others. The merits of individual cases will be taken into account. Hyundai was given the go-ahead because its proposal began with 78% indigenization, which by the year 2000 is projected to increase to 98%. A proposal by the American cosmetics giant Avon was cleared even though some of its operations were in areas reserved for the small-scale sector. This is because the company promised to provide employment for least 1,000 women to market its products.

Policy Change

Foreign firms in India have normally taken equity positions only in high technology industries and in areas where brand names are involved. Joint ventures in commodity-based industrial sectors have often been technical collaborations without financial involvement. In a recent policy decision, the FIPB decided that foreign companies would also be allowed to set up 100% subsidiaries in the consumer goods sector. The companies would first have to divest to enlarge the domestic equity base within a specified period.

MNCs' Side of the Story

One reason for MNCs setting up 100% subsidiaries is that when they have a certain proprietary technology and do want not share it, the technology stays better protected if they have a 100% ownership. In other words, 100% subsidiaries help MNCs retain proprietary control over technologies and products. Sometimes, these subsidiaries are set up for specialized purposes, for example, exports (Timex is planning to set up a fully-owned subsidiary to serve as a manufacturing base for its global operations). Another reason may be to integrate vertically backwards or forwards in order to gain economies of scale.

The setting up of such subsidiaries, however, is severely criticised in the case of MNCs already publicly quoted in India. For example, even though Cadbury Schweppes has a publicly quoted 51% subsidiary in India, Cadbury India Ltd, it set up a 100% subsidiary, Cadbury Schweppes Beverages India Pvt Ltd, to launch its Schweppes soft drink range in India. Similarly, Gillette now markets most of its new products through a fully owned subsidiary rather than through its existing company, which has Indian public shareholding. It is alleged that these companies are taking advantage of the recognition factor created by their Indian ventures to sell products (via the subsidiaries), subsequently pocketing the profits.

Preparing the Team

It is important to note that when a company selects a person to handle its business in a foreign country, the person should try to familiarise himself or herself with the historical, political, economic and social conditions of the host country. Many expatriate managers experience culture shock when they visit a developing country for the first time. A senior executive at GE sums it up best: "You've got to be prepared mentally to work in a challenging, not-so-streamlined environment [in which] certain inefficiencies such as low productivity, poor transport and power shortages will take a few years to iron out. You have to stay three years before life gets exciting."

Courses for Adjustment

Many organisations provide some kind of pre-departure expatriate training to executives to enhance their effectiveness in India. Courses focus on the cultural, social and business customs of the country. They help prepare managers for a smoother transition into the new country and also help create better-adapted managers who have more chances of success in business. Sometimes, however, what has been taught in these courses, though generally right on track, may not equip managers well enough for their particular assignment.

In one particular case, the managing director of Goodyear India, decided to do some pre-departure training on his own but failed to take into account an important factor—the region he was being posted to. Before leaving for India, he learnt some Hindi. However, he was posted to Chennai where the language widely spoken is Tamil. "I'd been taking lessons in Hindi. But I'm totally lost in Chennai," he said in jest.

Understanding the Market
The National Council for Applied Economic Research estimated that India's consumer class totalled 100 million (earlier estimation was 250 million) in 1997. There is much stratification among the consumers: different states have different consumption and behavioural patterns. Such complexities give entrenched players a big advantage.

New entrants would be better prepared if they come expecting a country of diversity, where the culture is complex and takes time to be fully understood. It must also be borne in mind that sometimes, there is a long waiting period for payback from the consumer market. Some multinational companies have burnt their fingers expecting quick returns from a consumer market they did not understand or assumed would be the same as everywhere else.

Life for the Expatriates
Many managers who come to India to work without any inkling of the state of affairs in the developing world have expressed their fear of the potential hardships they may face. The very same people, once adjusted to life in India, find it a truly enriching experience.

With its large metropolitan cities, India offers conveniences that are available in most parts of the developed world. It also offers the expatriate the additional advantage of low living costs, allowing them to afford luxuries, such as domestic help, chauffeur-driven cars and an inexpensive laundry service (*dhobi*, a home delivery service for washing and ironing clothes).

Indian Standard Time

Indians are hospitable and love inviting their friends and business associates to dinner. They also like to show off their "foreign connections" to others. They are generally known to be unpunctual for appointments.

At parties in Indian homes, hosts and hostesses usually do not expect their first guests to arrive at least half an hour after the stated time, unless they have explicitly requested otherwise. Knowing this practice would help expatriate managers avoid turning up too early and putting themselves and the hosts in an awkward situation. However, it never hurts to ask the hosts the exact time to turn up.

The following order is usually adhered to at parties: drinks, food and a quick goodbye. Many expatriates used to the reverse rule of a meal followed by an after-dinner drink often find that the best way to keep their stomachs from rumbling is to first have an early meal at home and then partake of the late meal served at the Indian homes.

Transportation Woes

The public transportation system is overstretched. The sheer volume of traffic, a variety of vehicles on the roads (from handcarts to autorickshaws, heavy vehicles, and cars), throngs of people and a generally poor transportation infrastructure lead to high transit times and commuter "wear out".

Many Indians cannot afford cars and the necessity to economise on conveyance/transport costs forces them to use multiple forms of transport to get to places (e.g. on foot or by bus, suburban train or autorickshaw). Many feel that the problems posed by the transportation system contribute to the observed phenomenon of "unpunctuality".

Working with Indians

Finding suitably qualified business managers to work for you is a major problem in an exploding business environment. While India has a large population base and there are many skilled and unskilled workers and middle level professionals with technical and managerial skills, the current number of senior business managers do not have adequate experience in the global marketplace. Hence, business managers with global experience are difficult to find. One way around this problem is to conduct a variety of training programmes for managers trying to break new ground in a multi-cultural and "think global" business environment. With the opening up of the economy and large numbers of MNCs setting up shop in India, there has been a growth in the number of human resource firms specialising in headhunting for companies.

An expatriate usually integrates successfully into the Indian way of life after a few weeks of arrival and finds it easy working with his Indian counterparts.

Indian business people are generally flexible in their dealings with investors. At the personal level, they are reasonably comfortable working with people of any nationality. English, the language of business, aids their communication with foreign investors. Knowing a little Hinglish—a mixture of Hindi and English—is a definite asset for the foreigner in India. However, there are various forms of Hinglish spoken in India. It is good to familiarise yourself with the subtleties and differences in pronunciation and accents that indicate the geographical and ethnic origins of the speakers

Some Useful Words and Phrases

English	Hindi
Good morning/afternoon/evening	Namaste (with palms joined together) [Nah-mes-TAY]
How are you?	Ap kaise hain? [AAP KAY-say heyn?]
My name is …	Mera nam … hai [MAY-ra NAAM … hey]
I have come from …	Main … se aya hun [MAIYN … say ayah HOOHN] (male) [MAIYN … say ai HOOHN] (female)
Yes	Han [HAHN]
No	Nahin; na [Na-HEEHN; NA]
Excuse me	Maf Karna [MAAF KAR-nah]
Thank you	Shukriya [SHOOK-ree-yah]
All right/Goodbye	Achchha [ATCH-chah]

Indians are good at negotiating deals. Although highly "collectivist" in their family or trading group, Indians show individuality and brilliance when negotiating on their own. This potential of theirs should be tapped by a foreign investor.

Be Prepared for Hiccups

While working on a project, one senior executive in India felt that at the lower level management of a company, people were unaware of the need to be efficient and productive, as well as the advancements made in information technology. He felt this lack of knowledge hindered their work progress. He eventually had a meeting with them to set things straight.

Dress Code

The different styles of Indian clothing reflect the geographical, ethnic and religious backgrounds of the wearers. As far as business is concerned, there is no strict dress code. Indians are generally conservative about dressing, except in the metropolitan cities of Mumbai and New Delhi, where women, for instance, sport cropped T-shirts and designer jeans, and as far as business is concerned, the latest "power suits".

Perhaps the most valuable piece of advice that can be given to a business person unfamiliar with India's business environment is this: dress conservatively. Women, for instance, are expected to dress modestly with their legs and shoulders covered. Trousers are acceptable, but short skirts and culottes are best left in the cupboards.

Business Cards

The lingua franca of business being English, most business cards are in this language. Occasionally a card is in a foreign language, for example, the card of a foreign representative who has an office in India. A business card is generally offered with courtesy and is intended to reflect the status of the person giving it in. The job title and qualifications of the giver are sometimes extensively spelt out on the card.

Often on business cards, the various ex-officio honorary positions that a business person holds (his/her membership in professional institutes, trade bodies, universities, etc. and his/her directorship on various companies) are explicitly stated. However, at the sophisticated business level, a simple business card that states the business person's highest academic qualification and company name will suffice.

Office Hours

Commercial offices in the private sector operate from around 9 a.m. to 5.30 p.m. The trade or the wholesale markets, such as the cloth markets, operate from around 11 a.m. to 8 p.m. The government sectors operate from 10 a.m. to 5 p.m. Many commercial establishments follow the practice of working only on the first and third Saturdays of every month. Banks usually operate from 9.30 a.m. to 2.30 p.m. for public transactions and are open until 5.30 p.m. for office work. Many central and state government offices keep to a five-day week.

The Media

The media in India is well developed, particularly the print media. India has a long history of a strong and free press, guarding and nurturing a vibrant democracy. One of the largest circulating English dailies *The Times of India* was established in 1838. During the emergency (1975 to 1977), there was government censorship of the media. The pressure the government exerts on the media when it gets too critical of the former is largely indirect. For example, it cuts down on the number of advertisements sponsored and discourages the public sector from publishing in anti-government media. Ramnath Goenka, the outspoken media baron

Workers leaving their office in the evening. For the female workers, the demands on them at work and the responsibilities at home have proven quite difficult to handle. Despite this, many have entered the job market.

of the Indian Express Group, however, was relentless in his attacks on the Congress Party until his death recently.

Radio programmes, until lately, were largely monopolised by the government-owned All India Radio. There are now several FM stations run by media companies, which broadcast music programmes for the young and business programmes and interviews for executives.

There has recently been an explosion in the Indian television scene. There are many private television channels operating in India. Since the entry of satellite channels and cable television into India, Indians have been lapping up Western music and programmes. This has had a dramatic impact on their awareness about the goods and services available around the world and created a keen sense of competition among manufacturers. Indians have become more discerning in their purchasing decisions. Product quality is now an important determinant.

Schools

There is a large number of public schools in India that provide quality education. Convent schools (where English is the main medium of instruction) and American schools are also abundant in major Indian cities, as are language schools teaching Japanese, French, Italian and German. Play schools following the Montessori system, for instance, are found in the cities and are of a high standard.

Professional Services

India offers a number of high-quality professional services. These include law firms, management consultancy firms, accounting and auditing firms, advertising agencies and many others (some of them even date back to the pre-independence era). Many firms now have affiliations with international organisations. Recently, the field of management consultancy has seen a dramatic increase in new players.

Patents, Trademarks and Copyright Laws

Patents, trademarks and copyright laws in India have been lax in the past. However, with the completion of the Uruguay Round of the GATT agreement and the signing of the WTO agreement in 1996, India is within bounds of the international requirements of the agreement. There is now, unlike in the past, a fairly effective means of enforcing the laws on patents and copyrights.

Staff Leave Entitlement

Employees are entitled to about 25 working days of privilege leave every year. It is expected to be planned in advance. Casual leave,

Some foreigners spend their leisure time doing what they like best—shopping. Handicraft, antique and clothes stores on the streets are the best places for bargains.

taken at short notice for emergencies, is between five to seven working days, while sick leave can be taken for five to seven days.

Public Holidays

There are public holidays for the major festivals of all communities. Independence Day, Republic Day, Mahatma Gandhi's birthday, Diwali, Eid and Christmas are major national holidays. Local states have specific holidays based on the importance of their local festivals.

Leisure

Many expatriates are members of various Indian associations and trade groups, where they learn the ropes of Indian business culture and social behaviour. They have easy access to the old colonial clubs in the country, which are the watering holes of the elite. There are also special groups for the wives of expatriates that help them adjust to life in an unfamiliar country. Indus in Mumbai is one such group. If they so desire, the wives of expatriates can get a job, but they must be realistic enough not to expect the same salary they were used to in their home countries.

CHAPTER 9

India's Foreign Trade

India's trade links with the rest of the world have increased over the years. In keeping with the current trend towards globalisation, India has taken major initiatives to diversify its export base. It now exports around 7,500 commodities to 190 countries and imports 600 commodities from around 140 countries.

Exports cover a wide range of items from the agricultural, industrial, handicraft, handloom and cottage sectors. Project exports such as consultancy, civil construction and turn-key contracts have seen a significant increase in recent years, as have electronic, hardware and software exports.

In April 1987, India adopted the Customs Co-operation Council's harmonised commodity description and coding system for trade classification. The system was extended to meet domestic needs, thereby making it possible to record trade information more clearly.

Value and Direction of Foreign Trade

India conducts bilateral negotiations with both developing and developed countries. This gives it extensive export and import trade links. Imports and exports at current prices have risen from $1 billion to around $26 to 28 billion over the 50 years since independence.

However, India's international trade has grown dramatically in absolute, but not relative, values. The country has only had a modest 2% of global trade over the last three decades. Although its exports have grown considerably in the last few years, India's imports are still higher than its exports (see table that follows), resulting in a balance of payment deficit.

Key Statistics of the Indian Economy			
	Exports	Imports	Exports as % of Imports
1950–1951	606*	608	99.7
1960–1961	642	1,122	57.2
1970–1971	1,535	1,634	93.9
1980–1981	6,711	12,549	53.5
1990–1991	32,553	43,198	75.4
1993–1994	69,751	73,101	95.4
1994–1995	82,674	89,971	91.9
1995–1996	106,465	121,647	87.5

*Rs in crore

Source: Statistical Outline of India, 1996–1997

Changing Pattern of Foreign Trade

There have been several significant developments in India's foreign trade in recent years. Exports have shown impressive growth in terms of commodities and markets, while imports have been regulated so as to facilitate an easier flow of raw materials and capital goods into the country.

Imports

Imports help meet the essential requirements of domestic consumption, investment and production. Bulk imports, such as fertilizers, newsprint, petrol and petroleum products, account for roughly 40% of total imports. Other principal imports include pearls, precious and semi-precious stones, machinery, project goods, medicinal and pharmaceutical products, organic and inorganic chemicals, coal, coke and briquettes, and artificial resins. Imports, such as cereals, registered a decline in the period 1995 to 1996.

Export Promotion

India's overall trade strategy is to move away from sector-specific subsidies and physical controls towards macro-level fiscal controls and incentives. A realistic management of the exchange rate is also deemed necessary.

The trade strategy includes policy measures for export-linked imports, the phased reduction of import licensing, the strengthening of export incentives, the introduction of market-determined exchange rates, greater availability of export credit at lower interest rates, as well as the reduction and restructuring of import duties. In addition, state governments will be more involved in implementing these policies. In keeping with the move towards a promotional regime, infrastructural facilities will be strengthened and procedural irritants removed by simplifying and streamlining policies and their methods of implementation. States are being involved in export promotion efforts through such schemes as the Export Promotion Industrial Park Scheme (EPIP).

Foreign Trade Over the Years

	Imports	Exports	Balance
1950–1951	608*	606	-2
1960–1961	1,122	642	-480
1970–1971	1,634	1,535	-99
1980–1981	12,549	6,711	-5838
1985–1986	19,658	10,895	-8,763
1990–1991	43,198	32,553	-8,763
1991–1992	47,851	44,041	-3,810
1992–1993	63,375	53,688	-9,687
1993–1994	73,101	69,751	-3,350
1994–1995	89,971	82,674	-7,297
1995–1996	121,647	106,465	-15,182

*Rs in crore
Source: India Development Report, 1997

Import Policy

Capital goods, raw materials, intermediates, components, consumables, spare parts, accessories, instruments and other goods may be imported without any restriction unless regulated by the Negative List of Imports, which places restrictions on certain goods on the grounds of public policy.

Goods that require no licensing may be imported by any person regardless of whether or not that person is the actual user. However, goods that require a licence may only be imported by the actual user alone. This condition holds unless the licensing authorities specifically dispense with it.

Except for items on the Negative List of Imports, consumer durables, components, spare parts and accessories may be imported without a licence, subject to the actual user condition. All second-hand capital goods with a minimum residual life of five years may also be imported without a licence, again subject to the actual user condition. All other second-hand goods may be imported in accordance with a public notice or a licence issued in this regard.

Export-Import Policy

The Export-Import Policy is effective for a period of five years from 1 April 1992 to 31 March 1997 and runs parallel with the Eighth Plan period. The fundamental feature of the new policy is freedom of foreign trade. Licensing, quantitative restrictions and other regulatory and discretionary controls have been reduced considerably.

All goods may be imported and exported freely, save for those on the Negative List of Imports and Negative List of Exports. An important feature of the revised policy is the broad scope of the Export Promotion Capital Goods (EPCG) scheme, which provides a zero-duty import on capital goods with a value of at least Rs20 crore. There are options for fulfilling the export obligation either on an FOB or a net foreign exchange earning (NFE) basis. Coverage of the scheme is extended to merchant exporters and all service providers.

Indian Missions

There are currently 66 commercial offices attached to Indian missions abroad, including the office of the Ambassador of India to the WTO. The ambassador is also the permanent representative of India to the United Nations Conference on Trade and Development (UNCTAD). Recently, a commercial office was set up in Johannesburg, South Africa.

Offices functioning under the control of the Ministry of Commerce play a vital role in promoting India's foreign trade and economic relations. Through regular feedback on the global economic situation, market trends and trade promotion prospects, commercial representatives assist the Indian government in formulating trade and economic policies. A monthly newsletter published by the Ministry of Commerce keeps the commercial representatives abreast of the latest economic developments. The ministry has also introduced computerised database-reporting to facilitate the function of the commercial offices. It has also increased the budget for the commercial offices.

India Takes On the World

South Asia

India's trade with its neighbours, Afghanistan, Bangladesh, Bhutan, Maldives, Nepal, Pakistan and Sri Lanka, has been growing rapidly in recent years. Its two-way trade with these countries represents 2 to 3% of its global trade turnover. Bangladesh is India's largest trading partner, followed by Sri Lanka.

Southeast Asia and Australia

Despite good trade links with most of the countries in Southeast Asia, India has not fully exploited the boom preceding the economic crisis that plagued the region from 1997. Hong Kong, Singapore, Thailand and Australia are major destinations for India's exports. Australia, Singapore, Malaysia and the Republic of Korea account for most of its imports.

Japan
India's trade with Japan constitutes 7 to 9% of its total global trade. India's major exports to Japan include spices, cashew nuts, iron ore, gems and jewellery, dyes and intermediaries, handicrafts, tea, coffee, castor oil, marine products, leather goods, drugs and pharmaceuticals, paints and enamels, cotton yarn, handmade carpets and processed minerals. Major imports include iron and steel, machine tools, synthetic rubber and fibres and textile yarns. Since 1996, Japan has been trying to establish closer economic ties with India and promote direct investment (by private companies) in the country. If all goes well, India will be a big market for Japanese automobiles and other products.

The Middle East and Africa
West Asian and North African countries are important to India's trade. The balance of trade, however, is not in India's favour because it imports large quantities of crude oil from this region. The Middle East and Africa are also important sources of industrial raw materials like fertilizers and rock phosphate. The region is a promising market for India's exports in engineering, agriculture, gems and jewellery. India has trade agreements with Egypt, Iraq, Iran, Afghanistan, Jordan, Kuwait, Libya, Morocco, Syria and Tunisia.

India has also taken several measures to increase bilateral co-operation and joint ventures with the sub-Saharan African countries. Major measures undertaken include exchanging trade delegations at the ministerial and official levels, holding joint committee or joint commission meetings, participating in fairs and exhibitions and organising exclusive Indian fairs. Trade agreements have so far been signed with 15 countries: Angola, Cameroon,

Ethiopia, Ghana, Ivory Coast, Kenya, Liberia, Mozambique, Nigeria, Rwanda, Senegal, Uganda, Zaire, Zambia and Zimbabwe.

Trade with South Africa was re-established in October 1993 after a lapse of four decades. Major export items to this region are engineering goods, transportation equipment, cotton garments and linen, chemicals and allied products, tobacco and spices. Major imports include copper, lead, zinc, cobalt, rock phosphate, phosphoric acid, raw cashew nuts, asbestos, pulses, fluorspar, wattle extract and other tanning and dyeing materials.

Western Europe

Another major trading area Western Europe accounts for about 25 to 30% of India's total exports and about 30 to 35% of its imports. The region includes countries in the European Union (the United Kingdom, Belgium, Denmark, France, Greece, Ireland, Italy, Luxembourg, the Netherlands, Spain and Portugal), countries of the European Free Trade Association (Austria, Finland, Norway, Sweden, Switzerland, Iceland and Liechtenstein) and Turkey, Malta and Cyprus.

Eight countries dominate India's total exports to Western Europe. They are Germany, the United Kingdom, Belgium, Italy, France, the Netherlands, Spain and Switzerland. Most of the other markets in the region are relatively unexplored. The main export items are textiles, yarn fabrics, garments, leather and leather goods, gems and jewellery, carpets, engineering goods and agricultural and marine products. Imports from this region are generally manufactured products, especially industrial plant and equipment, chemicals, steel and transport equipment.

India has trade agreements with several European countries. An important one is the new Indian-European Agreement on Partnership and Development. India-EC bilateral and economic relations recently came up for review at the meetings of the Joint Commissions/Committees.

Eastern Europe

India's trade with the 27 countries of Eastern Europe (formerly the Rupee Payment Area) has been positive since 1993. There was a dramatic decline in trade in the period 1991 to 1992 because of political changes in the East European region.

Various agreements on bilateral trade and economic matters have recently been signed. These include agreements on tourism, the environment, merchant shipping and long-term purchases of certain commodities from debt repayment funds. With the exception of Azerbaijan, relations have been established on a new footing with all the former states of the Soviet Union.

North America

The United States is India's largest single trading partner, representing around 8 to 10% of the country's global trade. India's major exports to the United States include gems and jewellery,

One of the many conferences in India that highlights the importance of the country integrating into the world economy.

ready-made garments, textiles, coir, jute and handicrafts, chemicals and allied products, engineering goods and leather and leather goods. Major imports from the United States include fertilizers, aircraft, turbojets, aircraft parts, automatic data processing machines, electronic goods, wood pulp and locomotive parts.

In December 1997, a US-India Trade Mission was held to promote trade opportunities between the two countries as well as to support the efforts of the US-India Commercial Alliance and US-India Business Council. The first-ever web site for a US trade mission was also launched the same month.

India's trade with Canada is modest, accounting for 0.5% of the country's global trade. Major export items include garments, leather goods, carpets, minerals, chemicals and allied products, coffee, cashew nuts, kernels, other types of nuts and spices. Major imports include pulp and waste paper, pulses, metalliferous ores and metal scraps, fertilizers, artificial resins, plastic materials, minerals, newsprint, non-ferrous metals, project goods and electrical machinery. With the liberalisation of India's economy, joint Indo-Canadian ventures in power generation, telecommunications, electronics, plastics, mining, automobile components, food processing and pharmaceuticals have either been formed or are in the offing.

South and Central America

India's exports to this region have been growing, although slowly, in recent years as a result of the lowering of tariffs and non-tariff barriers in many of the Latin American countries. Argentina, Brazil, Chile, Peru, Mexico, Panama, Colombia and Uruguay are India's major export markets in the region. Exports include textiles and ready-made garments, drugs and pharmaceuticals, engineering goods like bicycle diesel engines and handtools, leather and leather products and dye and dye intermediaries.

Imports include sugar, crude metals, iron and steel and their products, non-ferrous metals, metalliferous ores, vegetable oils, pulp and paper waste and raw wool. With a view to maximising export opportunities in the Latin American countries, India is contemplating promotional steps like posting commercial representatives to the region, participating in fairs and exhibitions there, sending trade delegations, and disseminating information and literature on Indian products in Spanish and Portuguese.

Basic Facts and Travel Tips

Accommodation

Accommodation is varied and cheap in India, from exclusive deluxe hotels boasting world-class facilities to ordinary budget hotels. Prices in major cities for luxury establishments with Western-style comforts and services are higher. As India does not have a particular tourist season, prices for most types of accommodation are the same throughout the year. Some resorts that are popular with tourists cost more. Many railway stations have retiring rooms for passengers to sleep. These are convenient if you are catching an early morning train but tend to get booked up well in advance. Although prices vary, they are generally the same as budget hotels. The rooms are large and clean.

Hotels

There are many affordable hotels in India. Prices start as low as Rs100 for a double room. Some hotels, on the periphery of big cities, charge even lower rates.

Some state governments run their own tourist resorts, similar to mid-range hotels, at stopover places on the highways. They are usually value for money, although prices vary significantly from state to state and even within states. Good hotels are expensive in Delhi and Mumbai, where prices are double those in other cities.

The grandeur of the Raj lingers in some hotels and club accommodation. In states like Rajasthan, Uttar Pradesh and Madhya Pradesh, old forts and palaces have been converted into hotels. The Taj Group (part of the Tata Enterprise in Mumbai) is the country's oldest hotel chain. Other reputable hotel chains include Oberoi, Holiday Inn, Meridien, Hyatt, Sheraton and the government-owned Ashoka chain. These hotels are found in most state capitals and in resorts frequented by wealthy Indian and foreign tourists.

Renting a Room

In some parts of India, you can rent a room in a house. This is a good idea if you are not planning to stay long in the country. In Rajasthan, the state tourist development corporation runs a Paying Guest Scheme that places tourists with families that offer lodging. The Munjita Travel in London, for instance, organises Homestay Hours across India. This is an excellent way of getting to know an Indian family and allows you to learn more about their way of life.

Climate

India has three major seasons: winter, summer and monsoon. The winter months are from November to March, while summer is from April to June. Summer is hot in most parts of India. The south west monsoon usually starts at the beginning of June on the west coast, reaching the northern areas later.

Communication

With the development of the telecommunications sector, both domestic and international calls can now be made directly in all cities. Phone services with international direct dialling facilities or STD/ISD services are available in most cities and even rural areas. For many Indians living in cities like Mumbai and New Delhi, fax and e-mail are very much part of their lives.

Crime Rate

The crime rate in India is well below those in some countries. However, you must take some precautions. It is advisable to call for a taxi from a known taxi company rather than hailing one of the stray cabs cruising the streets at night. Pickpockets generally wander crowded areas, such as trains, buses and busy railway stations, as do purse and chain snatchers. To avoid credit card frauds, insist that transactions be processed in your presence.

Currency Regulations

There is no restriction on the amount of foreign currency or traveller's cheques a visitor may bring into India. However, a currency declaration form has to be filled if more than US$10,000 or the equivalent in any foreign currency is brought into the country.

Duty-free Allowance

Anyone over 18 years of age can bring in US 1 quart (0.95 litres) of spirits or a bottle of wine and 250 ml spirits plus 200 cigarettes or 50 cigars or 250 grams of tobacco. A traveller is required to register all valuables taken out of the country by declaring them on a Tourist Baggage Re-export Form.

Electricity

Personal appliances and electronic equipment from the United States and a few other countries will not work in India without a transformer. Domestic electric current is 220 volts 50 cycles AC.

Foreign Exchange Dealers

Foreign currency may be converted through banks or authorised money changers, which are located in all international airports and cities. Not all banks change foreign currencies and traveller's cheques other than the greenback or the sterling pound. Private foreign exchange companies are located in various parts of the country.

Getting To and Around

India's international carrier, Air India, operates services to major destinations around the world. Its major domestic carrier, Indian

Airlines, provides services to 72 destinations, including 12 neighbouring countries. There are many private airlines operating in the country. Furthermore, a number of international airlines provide flights to major cities of the world from Mumbai, Delhi, Chennai, Bangalore and Calcutta. Many shipping, air cargo, and courier services also operate to and from India, which is five and a half hours ahead of Greenwich Mean Time.

It is convenient to travel across India. Major cities are serviced by Indian Airlines (a shuttle flight exists for the four main metropolitan cities of Mumbai, New Delhi, Calcutta and Chennai), the national carrier and a few other private airlines companies. When on a business trip and time is of the essence, taking a flight is a better alternative as it is a much quicker way of getting to your destination. The Delhi-Bangalore sector, from the north to the south of India, takes as long as 36 hours by train and only one and a half hours by plane.

With the world's largest network of railways (some even extending to the rural and remote areas of the country), travelling by train is one of the greatest experiences in India—it is simply unparalleled. Most train stations in India have "cloakrooms" for passengers to leave their luggage, for which you are required to produce a train ticket or Indrail pass (similar to the Eurorail pass) to retrieve them. It is advisable to keep track of the operating hours of the cloakroom to ensure that it is open when you need to collect your bags or suitcases. There are ladies' compartments on all overnight trains and even on most local trains. Some stations also have "ladies only" waiting rooms.

Most stations have computerized booking counters; hence, information about seats is immediately available. In the big cities, some stations have special compartments with English-speaking staff for foreigners. As the demand for train travel is high, it is important to plan your train journey in advance. With an Indrail pass, you can book tickets with Indian railways representatives stationed in your country. Your schedule should also be flexible enough to accommodate delays that may occur.

The Indian railways publishes an annual timetable that details the date, time and route of the express trains. It can be obtained from the information counters and newsstands at the main stations. Train schedules can be obtained from major terminals, but they are at times difficult to obtain.

Boat

Apart from river ferries, there are a few boat services in India. They are useful in crossing areas where bridges have yet to be constructed. The areas with any real cruiser services are the Andaman islands, Calcutta and Madras. There is also a cruiser service between Cochin and the Lakshadweep islands. In mainland India, the states with regular passenger boat services are Kerala and Calcutta.

Bus

Although the railway is the best way to experience India and is generally more comfortable than travelling by bus, there are some places not served by trains. Buses are also sometimes faster than trains. Luggage is carried either at the back of buses or on the roof. The bus ticket has the registration number of the bus and usually a seat number. Sometimes tickets can be bought on the bus itself.

Buses, however, vary somewhat in standards. Government-run buses, which cover short and long distances, are usually packed. In remote, yet widely travelled areas, there are private buses that are less crowded and more comfortable to travel. In many cities and towns, private tour operators run air-conditioned coaches to nearby tourist spots.

Car, Motorbike or Taxi

Driving in India is not for the fainthearted. Drivers take whatever liberties they can get away with. In India, like Britain, driving is done on the left side of the road. Traffic is heavy and undisciplined, with pedestrians, cyclists, rickshaws and cattle wandering on the roads. In the countryside, roads are narrow and dusty. Sometimes, bullock-carts or a herd of goats or cattle may cause a traffic jam. During the monsoon season, roads are often flooded and pose a danger to drivers. As roads are not usually clearly marked, it is best to stick to the main highways.

While it is possible to travel to distant places on cars, roads outside urban areas in some states are narrow and difficult to navigate during the monsoons. Foreigners are advised to take taxis, which are available at reasonable rates in most major cities and tourist areas. On overnight trips, the driver usually sleeps in the car or a motel. Car rental companies also supply chauffeur-driven vehicles. The best deals for self-drive rented cars are offered by big international chains. They cost 30% to 40% less than chauffeur-driven cars. Motorbikes or mopeds, popular in Goa, may be rented out in a few places.

The auto-rickshaw is a scooter with seats for passengers. It is cheaper than a taxi. Auto-rickshaws, however, are a little unstable, and the drivers can be reckless. It is always best to ask your driver to go at a slow speed in any vehicle you hire. In Calcutta, rickshaws continue to be pulled by men on foot. If you want to see a variety of places around town, consider hiring a taxi, rickshaw or auto-rickshaw for the whole day. Find a driver who speaks English reasonably well and agree on a price beforehand. Travel and tourist guides may be purchased from bookstores in major tourist spots.

Health

Hot food and food that is boiled or fried in your presence is usually safe for consumption. Avoid raw meat and vegetables. It is generally not a good idea to drink tap water, although water is usually chlorinated in the big cities. Bottled mineral water and quality soft drinks and beer are now widely available. Always check the seal of bottles for the expiry dates.

The lack of proper sanitation in India is often exaggerated, but if you are well informed and prepared, you can prevent yourself from falling sick. Bear in mind that things like bacteria multiply far more quickly in a tropical climate. Have a medical checkup before leaving your country. Be extra careful about personal hygiene. Avoid sharing a razor with anyone. It is also not advisable to go around barefoot. In case you fall sick, most Indian cities have well-equipped hospitals for treatment. There are also many private clinics that boast highly qualified doctors. Do not be fooled by quacks.

All travellers to India from yellow fever zones are required by law to show proof of yellow fever vaccinations. This is the only health-related formality that needs to be fulfilled before entering the country. It is also advisable for you take typhoid and hepatitis A vaccinations with tetanus, polio and other boosters. You can get vaccinations in Delhi, Mumbai and other major cities if necessary. Vaccination against meningitis is also advised.

Diarrhoea and Heat Trouble

Diarrhoea is the most common travellers' complaint. It is usually the case of your stomach reacting to "unfamiliar" food. It usually clears within 24 to 48 hours without treatment. Dehydration is another problem that foreigners may face; hence, it is best to drink plenty of fluids in the summer.

HIV and AIDS
HIV levels are high among prostitutes in India, so it is unwise to engage in casual sex with them, even with contraceptives. You should also be careful about blood transfusions if at all the need arises.

Malaria
It is advisable to get protection against malaria. Consult a doctor in the case of a fever, and take preventive tablets before and after your trip. As the malaria parasite incubates for more than a month, it is absolutely necessary to continue taking preventive tablets for at least four weeks after returning home. If you intend to stay in India for a few years, go for a thorough medical checkup regularly.

Rabies
Cases of rabies are reported in some areas in India; hence, it is best to avoid playing with stray animals. A bite, scratch or even a lick from an infected animal could spread the disease. Wash such wounds immediately with soap or detergent and apply alcohol or iodine. Consult a doctor next.

Maps
Big bookstores have good maps of India. City maps are can be obtained from tourist offices.

Palace on Wheels
The Rajasthan Tourist Development Corporation runs Palace on Wheels, a luxury, air-conditioned train with accommodation that goes on weekly tours of Rajasthan. The Palace on Wheels, which operates between September and April, has been a big hit and seven similar train services are currently being developed to tour the different regions of the country. An interesting option similar to this is the tours run by British travel operators Butterfields in

specially converted carriages attached to a series of scheduled trains. These tours must be booked in the United Kingdom.

Special Permits

In addition to visas, special permits are required for certain parts of the country (notably parts of Sikkim, Ladakh, the Andaman islands, Lakshadweep and some north eastern hill states), while others (such as the cantonment area where the armed forces establishment is located) remain out of bounds to foreign nationals. If you have a special reason for going to the areas that require special permits, you should apply for a permit at the Ministry of Home Affairs (Foreigners' Section) four weeks in advance.

Tipping

Tipping takes various forms, the commonest of which is rewarding a waiter or porter for services rendered. Taxi drivers and staff at some hotels and restaurants do not expect tips. Some taxi drivers, however, are known to demand tips from foreigners. Paying people for favours, especially for speeding up bureaucratic processes is common and is not perceived as bribery.

Foreigners' Regional Registration Offices	
Calcutta	9/1, Gariahat Road, Calcutta — 700 020. Tel: 44 3301, 2470549.
Chennai	9, Village Road, Nungabakkam, Chennai — 600 034. Tel: 8277036.
Mumbai	2nd Floor, 414 V.S. Marg, Prabhadevi, Mumbai — 400 001. Tel: 4301331.
New Delhi	Ist Floor, Hans Bhavan, Tilak Bridge, New Delhi — 110 002. Tel: 3391781.

In addition, the superintendents of police in all district headquarters function as registration officers for foreigners.

Visas

All non-Indian citizens are required to obtain a visa. Visitors' visas are the easiest to obtain for trips that span six months. Business visas, which can be issued for a maximum of five years with provisions for multiple entry, are useful for business executives who wish to visit India frequently. Foreigners, who intend to work in India for a year or less, can apply for multiple entry employment visas.

A foreigner who wishes to stay in India for more than 180 days needs a residential permit. These can be obtained within 14 days of arrival in India from one of the Foreigners Regional Registration Offices in the four metropolitan cities or from the Foreigners Office of the state in which he/she wishes to stay. The permits take two or three days to be issued.

The best place to obtain a visa is the Indian Embassy or High Commission in your home country. It is also possible in some countries to pay a travel agency to obtain a visa on your behalf (this is sometimes faster). It is no longer possible to extend a visa in India, although exceptions may be made on a case by case basis.

Directory of Important Contacts

Some Useful Addresses

Reserve Bank of India (RBI)
Exchange Control Department
Central Office Building
Shaheed Bhagat Singh Road
Post Box No. 1055
Mumbai 400 023,
India
Tel: 91-22-266 3596
Fax: 91-22-266 5330, 266 2105,
265 4121

Secretariat for Industrial Approvals (SIA)
Department of Industrial
Development
Ministry of Industry
Udyog Bhavan
New Delhi 110 011,
India
Tel: 91-11-301 1983
Fax: 91-11-301 1770

Foreign Investment Promotion Board (FIPB)
Ministry of Industry
New Delhi 110 011, India
Tel: 91-11-301 1815, 301 1983
Fax: 91-11-301 6298

Securities and Exchange Board of India (SEBI)
Mittal Court, B Wing
224 Nariman Point
Mumbai 400 021, India
Tel: 91-22-204 5623
Fax: 91-22-202 1093

Chief Commissioner (Investment and NRIs)
India Investment Centre (IIC)
Jeevan Vihar, Sansad Marg
New Delhi 110 001, India
Tel: 91-11-373 3673
Fax: 91-11-373 2245

Director General, Foreign Trade (DGFT)
Udyog Bhavan
New Delhi 110 001, India
Tel: 91-11-301 1777
Fax: 91-11-301 1779

Joint Secretary
Investment Promotion Cell
Ministry of Power
Shram Shakti Bhawan, Rafi Marg
New Delhi 110 001
Tel: 91-11-371 0389
Fax: 91-11-371 7519

Sr. Dy. Director General
Customer Service
Sanchar Bhavan
20, Ashoka Road,
New Delhi 110 001
Tel: 91-11-303 2855, 91-11-332 6255
Fax: 91-11-332 7656

Joint Secretary
Industry Promotion Division
Department of Electronics
Electronics Niketan,
6 CGO Complex,
Lodi Road
New Delhi 110 003
Tel: 91-11-436 3101
Fax: 91-11-436 3101

Joint Secretary (Exploration)
Ministry of Petroleum and Natural Gas
Shastri Bhavan
Dr. Rajendra Prasad Marg
New Delhi 110 001
Tel: 91-11-386 935
Fax: 91-11-384 787

Joint Secretary (Refineries)
Ministry of Petroleum and Natural Gas
Shastri Bhavan
Dr. Rajendra Prasad Marg
New Delhi 110 001
Tel: 91-11-381 832
Fax: 91-11-384 787

Joint Secretary (Marketing)
Ministry of Petroleum and Natural Gas
Shastri Bhavan
Dr. Rajendra Marg
New Delhi 110 001
Tel: 91-11-381 052
Fax: 91-11-384 787

Joint Secretary
Ministry of Food Processing
Panchsheel Bhawan
Khel Gaon Marg
New Delhi 110 049
Tel: 91-11- 649 2476, 649 2475
Fax: 91-11-649 3228

Director
International Cooperation Cell
Ministry of Mines
Shastri Bhawan, New Delhi 110 001
Tel: 91-11-384 593
Fax: 91-11-386 402

Director General (Roads)
Ministry of Surface Transport
Transport Bhawan
1, Sansad Marg,
New Delhi 110 001
Tel: 91-11-371 5159
Fax: 91-11-371 0236

Joint Secretary (Ports)
Transport Bhawan
1, Parliament Street
New Delhi 110 001
Tel: 91-11-371 0140
Fax: 91-11-371 4324

Joint Secretary (Shipping)
Transport Bhawan
1, Parliament Street
New Delhi 110 001
Tel: 91-11-371 0189
Fax: 91-11-371 4324

Additional Director General
Department of Tourism
Transport Bhawan
1, Parliament Street
New Delhi 110 001
Tel: 91-11-371 5084
Fax: 91-11- 371 0518

Joint Secretary (PI)
Ministry of Chemicals
Shastri Bhavan
Dr. Rajendra Prasad Road
New Delhi 110 001
Tel: 91-11-385 131
Fax: 91-11-382 467

**Santa Cruz Electronics Export
Processing Zone**
Andheri (East)
Mumbai 400 096, India
Tel: 91-22-836 7143
Fax: 91-22-832 1169

Falta Export Processing Zone
2nd MSO Building
4th Floor, Room No. 4
Nizam Palace
234/4, A J C Bose Road
Calcutta 700 020, India
Tel: 91-33-247 7923
Fax: 91-33-247 2263

Cochin Export Processing Zone
CPZ Administrative Building
Kakkanad
Cochin 682 030, India
Tel: 91-484-422 530, 422 551
Fax: 91-484-422 530

Noida Export Processing Zone
PHD House, 3rd Floor
Khel Gaon Marg
New Delhi 110 016
India
Tel: 91-11-685 5061
Fax: 91-11-685 5061

Kandla Free Trade Zone
Gandhidham
Kutch 370 230, India
Tel: 91-2836-521 94
Fax: 91-2836-522 50

Madras Export Processing Zone
Administrative Building
GST Road, Tambaram
Chennai 600 045, India
Tel: 91-44-236 8220
Fax: 91-44-236 8218

**Visakhapatnam Export Processing
Zone**
Udyog Bhavan Complex, Shripuram
Junction
Visakhapatnam 530 003, India
Tel: 91-891-551 259, 554 577
Fax: 91-891-551 259
Telex: 0495334 VEPZ IN

The Industrial Credit and Investment Corporation of India Ltd. (ICICI)
163, Backbay Reclamation
Mumbai 400 020
Tel: 91-22-204 5190, 91-22-202 2535
Fax: 91-22-204 6582

Industrial Development Bank of India (IDBI)
IDBI Tower, Cuffe Parade
Colaba, Mumbai 400 005
Tel: 91-22-218 5320
Fax: 91-22-218 8137, 218 0411

Industrial Finance Corporation of India Ltd. (IFCI)
Bank of Baroda Building
16, Sansad Marg, New Delhi 110 001
Tel: 91-11-332 2052
Fax: 91-11-332 0425

Export Import Bank of India (EXIM)
P B 16100, Centre One
World Trade Centre, Cuffe Parade
Mumbai 400 005
Tel: 91-22-218 5272, 91-22-218 2255
Fax: 91-22-218 2690

Financial Institutions

Reserve Bank of India
(The Central Banking Authority)

Bombay
Central Office Bullding, Shahid Bhagat
Singh Road, Bombay - 400 001.
Tel : 22-2660502
Fax : 22-2660358

Calcutta
15, Netaji Subhash Road,
Calcuna - 700 001
Tel: 33-2208331
Fax: 33-2209589

Madras
Fort Glacis, Rajaji Salai,
Madras 600 001
Tel: 44-560211/562042/561923
Fax: 44-565220

New Delhi
6, Sansad Marg,
New Delhi-110 001
Tel: 11-3710538-42
Fax: 11-3711250

Export Credit Guarantee Corporation of India

Bangalore
RahejaTower, 11th Floor, West Wing,
26, M. G. Road, Bangalore-560 001.
Tel : 80-5589779
Fax : 80-5589779

Bombay
Express Towers, 10th Floor,
Nariman Point, Bombay - 400 021.
Tel : 22 -2885625/2885452
Fax: 22-2023267

Madras
Spencer Towers, 770-A Anna Salai
Madras 600 002.
Tel: 44-8522616/998
Fax: 44-8522537

Export-Import Bank of India

Bangalore
Ramanashree Arcade
4th Floor, 18, M. G. Road,
Bangalore-560 001
Tel: 80-5585755/9101
Fax: 80-5589107

Bombay
Maker Chambers IV, 222,
Nariman Point,
Bombay - 400 021.
Tel: 22-2830761/0793
Fax: 22-2022132

Calcutta
5A & 5B, Park Plaza, 71, Park Street,
Calcutta - 700 016
Tel: 33-292467/293416
Fax: 33-2269357

Madras
UTI House, 1st Floor,
29, Rajaji Salai, Madras-600 001
Tel: 44-5224714/49
Fax: 44-5224082

New Delhi
Tower 1, Jeevan Bharati Bldg
8th Floor, 124, Connaught Circus
New Delhi-110 001
Tel: 11-3326375/6625
Fax: 11-3322758/1719

Industrial Credit & Investment Corporation of India Ltd.

Bangalore
Raheja Tower, 2nd Floor, East Wing,
26-25, M.G. Road,
Bangalore - 560 001
Tel: 80-5588536/5550049
Fax: 80-5588556

Bombay
ICICI Building, 163, Backbay Reclamation,
Churchgate, Bombay - 400 020.
Tel: 22-2022535/2022594
Fax: 22-2046582

Madras
1, Cenotaph Road, Madras - 600 018
Tel: 44-4344217/6375
Fax: 44-4342588

Industrial Development Bank of India

Bangalore
36, Cunningham Road,
Bangalore - 560 052
Tel: 79-2268131

Madras
480, Anna Salai, Madras - 600 035
Tel: 44-4331006/4330007

Industrial Reconstruction Bank of India

Bombay
IDBI Tower, Cuffe Parade,
Bombay - 400 005
Tel: 22-2189111/2189117
Fax: 22-2188137/2180411

Calcutta
19, N.S.C. Bose Road,
Calcutta - 700 001.
Tel: 33-2209941
Fax: 33-2207182

Madras
769, Anna Salai, Madras - 600 002
Tel: 44-8521536/8524912

Industrial Financial Corporation of India

Bangalore
3, Cubbonpet Main Road, N.R.Square,
Bangalore 560 002
Tel: 80-2211623/2210882

Madras
142, Uthamar Gandhi Salai,
Madras - 600 034
Tel : 44-8276569

New Delhi
Bank of Baroda Building,
16, Sansad Marg,
New Delhi 110 001
Tel: 11-332 1013
Fax: 11-332 0425

Life Insurance Corporation of India

Bangalore
Jeevan Prakash, J.C.Raod
Bangalore - 560 002
Tel: 80-2222191,
Fax: 80-2223179

Bombay
Yogakshema, Jeevan Bima Marg,
Bombay 400 021
Tel: 22-2022151/2021383
Fax: 22-2028943/2020274

Madras
102, Anna Salai, Madras - 600 002
Tel: 44-830556
Fax: 44-8544961

National Housing Bank

Bombay
Bombay Life Bldg.,
45, Veer Nariman Road,
Bombay 400 023.
Tel: 22-2851560/61/62/63
Fax: 22-2851555

Shipping Credit Investment Corporation of India Ltd.

Bombay
141, MakerTower, Cufle Parade,
Bombay 400 005.
Tel: 22-2180800
Fax: 22-2181539/1739

Small Industries Development Bank of India

Bombay
Nariman Bhavan,
227, Vinay K Shah Marg,
Nariman Point, Bombay 400 021.
Tel: 22-2851274/2851278/1280
Fax: 22-2044448

Calcutta
11, Dr. U N Brahmachari Street
Opp L.A. Martinari Girls School
Calcutta - 700 017
Tel: 33-2479809/2404183
Fax: 33- 2404093

Madras
476, Anna Salai,
Madras - 600 035
Tel: 44-4330286/0964

New Delhi
YMC Cultural Centre,
1, Jai Singh Road, PB.No.192,
New Delhi - 110 001
Tel: 11-336 4037/67
Fax: 11-374 7120

Trade and Industry Organisations

All India Manufacturers' Organisation

Bombay
4th Floor, Jeevan Sahakar,
Sir P M. Road, Bombay 400 001
Tel: 22-2661016/1272/4241
Fax: 22-2660838

Calcutta
West Bengal State Board of AIMO,
Llaco House, 1/3 Braborne Road,
Calcutta - 700 001
Tel: 33-220855

Madras
TamilNadu State Board of AIMO
High Road, Round Table House
69, Nungambakkam
Madras - 600 034
Tel: 44-8271966/8263162

New Delhi
DHP Regional Board Of AIMO,
AIMO House, E1/11, Jhandewalan
Extension, New Delhi -110 055
Tel: 11-528848

Associated Chamber of Commerce & Industry of India

Delhi
Allahabad Bank Bldg
17, Parliament St.
New Delhi 110 001.
Tel: 11-310704
Fax: 11-312193 .

Bombay Chamber of Commerce & Industry

Bombay
Mackinnon Mackenzie Bldg.,
4, Shoorji Vallabhdas Marg,
Ballard Est., Bombay 400 001.
Tel: 22-2614681/2/3/4
Fax: 22-2621213

Confederation of Indian Industry

Bangalore
Manipal Centre, 47,
Dickenson Road,
Bangalore - 560 042
Tel: 80-5583967
Fax: 80-5586106

Bombay
105, Kakad Chambers,
Worli, Bombay 400 018.
Tel: 22-4931790
Fax: 22-4939463/4945831

Calcutta
6, N.S. Road, Calcutta - 700 001
Tel: 33-2207727/1721

Madras
13, Harrington Road,
Chetpet
Madras - 600 031
Tel: 44-8279587/8270218
Fax: 44-8270218/9587

New Delhi
23,26 Institutional Area, Lodhi Road,
New Delhi -110 003
Tel: 11-4629994
Fax: 11-4626149/4633168

Federation of Indian Chambers of Commerce & Industry

New Delhi
Federation House, Tansen Marg,
New Delhi 110 001.
Tel: 11-3319251/33/9261
Fax: 11-3320714

Federation of Indian Export Organisations

Bombay
World Trade Centre No. 1,
11th Floor,
Cuffe Parade, Bombay 400 005.
Tel: 22-2185093/2183354
Fax: 22-2183875

Calcutta
Express Tower 42A, 6th Floor
Shakespeare Sarani,
Calcutta - 700 071
Tel: 33-2406398/4254
Fax: 33-2470364

Madras
Unit No 706, Spencer Plaza,
Anna Salai, Madras - 600 002
Tel: 44-8522427/1861
Fax : 44-8524767

New Delhi
PHD House, 3rd Floor,
Opp Asian Games Village Complex,
New Delhi-110 016
Tel: 11-6851310/12/14/15
Fax: 11-6863087

India Trade Promotion Organisation

Bangalore
Flat No.24-A, Imperiai Court
31/1, Cunningham Road,
Bangalore -560 052
Tel: 80-2268867/2266869
Fax: 80-2258662

Bombay
Jhansi Castle,
7, Cooperage Road,
Bombay - 400 039
Tel: 22-2021730/788
Fax: 22-2044922 .

Calcutta
Shantiniketan Flat No. 9,
4th Floor, 8, Camac Street.
Calcutta - 700 017
Tel: 33-2425820
Fax: 33-2428269

Kanpur
127/W-7/69 1st Floor,
Saket Nagar,
Kanpur - 208 014
Tel: 512-279051.
Fax: 512- 279051

Madras
Raja Annamalal Building,
2nd Floor, 18-A,
Rukmani Lakshmipathi Road,
Egmore, Madras - 600 008
Tel: 44-8554655
Fax: 44-8554740 .

New Delhi
Pragati Bhawan, Pragati Maidan
New Delhi -110 001
Tel: 11-3318143
Fax: 11-3318142/7896

Indian Merchants' Chambers

Bombay
IMC Bldg.,
Indian Merchant Chamber Marg,
Churchgate, Bombay 400 020.
Tel: 22-2046633
Fax: 22-2048508

Indian Investment Centre
Jeevan Vihar Building,
Sansad Marg, New Delhi - 110 00,
Tel: 11-3733673
Fax: 11-3732245

The Council of EEC Chambers of Commerce in India

Bombay
Y. B. Chavan Centre, 111 Floor,
General Jagannath Bhosale Marg,
Nariman Point, Bombay 400 020
Tel: 22-2826064/65
Fax: 22-2885403/04

Some Major Indian Banks

Allahabad Bank
Central Office:
2, N.S. Road,
Calcutta 700 001.
Tel: 2200283/3373
Fax: 2488323

International Division:
White House
119, Park Street
Calcutta 700 016
Tel: 292310/2363
Fax: 292363/5796

Andhra Bank
Central Office:
5-9-11, Saifabad,
Hyderabad 500 004
Tel: 2404801/240580
Fax: 240509

International Division:
Andhra Bank Building,
2nd Floor, Sultan Bazaar,
Hyderabad 500 195.
Tel: 4730985
Fax: 4730926

Bank of India
Central Office:
Express Towers,
Nariman Point,
Mumbai 400 021.
Tel: 2023020
Fax: 2024701

International Division:
Express Towers, 7th Floor,
Nariman Point,
Mumbai 400 021
Tel: 2023020
Fax: 2022831

Central Bank of India
Central Office:
Chandermukhi, 12th Floor,
Nariman Point,
Mumbai 400 021.
Tel: 2023942/2024393
Fax: 2028122

International Division:
Chandermukhi, 12th Floor,
Nariman Point,
Mumbai 400 021.
Tel: 2026776
Fax: 2044336

Indian Bank
Central Office:
31, Rajaji Salai,
Chennai 600 001.
Tel: 5231275
Fax: 5231285

International Division:
31, Rajaji Salai,
Chennai 600 001
Tel: 5231279

Indian Overseas Bank
Central Office:
763, Anna Salai,
Chennai 600 002.
Tel: 8523545/8524546
Fax: 85211 96/8524873

International Division:
763, Anna Salai,
Chennai 600 002.
Phone 852371 6
Fax: 8523395

State Bank of India
Central Office:
State Bank Bhavan,
Nariman Point,
Mumbai 400 021.
Phone 20227991/2025959
Fax: 2852708
Email:
pgk@mumbai.cobom.sbi.co.in

International Division:
State Bank Bhavan,
Nariman Point,
Mumbai 400 021.
Tel: 2028713
Fax: 2040073
Email:
tms@mumbai.cobom.sbi.co.in

SBI Capital Markets Ltd.
Central Office:
202, Maker Tower 'E',
Cuffe Parade
Mumbai 400 005.
Tel: 2189166-69
Fax: 2188332

United Bank of India
Central Office:
16, Old Court House Street,
Calcutta 700 001.
Tel: 2487471-5
Fax: 2485852

International Division:
16, Old Court House Street,
14th Floor, Calcutta 700 001.
Tel: 2486285
Fax: 2486922

Private Banks

Bank of Punjab Ltd
SCO 4647, Sector 9-D,
Madhya Marg,
Chandigarh.
Tel: 741196/743998
Fax: 743894

Corporate Office:
Ground Floor
Hemkunt Chambers,
89, Nehnu Place,
Nevv Delhi 110 019.
Phone: 6465430/31
Fax: 6465483

Centurion Bank Ltd.
1201, Raheja Centre,
Free Press Journal Marg,
Nariman Point
Mumbai 400 0Q1.
Phone: 2047234/2855914
Fax: 2845860

Global Trust Bank Ltd.
303-48-3 Sardar Patel Road,
Secunderabad 500 003.
Phone: 819190/81 9333
Fax: 819355/81 9255
Email: gtbl@hd1.vsnl.net.in

HDFC Bank Ltd.
Sandoz House,
Dr. Annie 8esant Road,
Worli, Mumbai 400 018.
Tel: 4951616
Fax: 4960737

ICICI Banking Corporation Ltd.
Zenith House, 3rd Floor,
Keshavrao Khade Marg,
Opp. Race Course,
Mahalaxmi,
Mumbai 400 011.
Tel: 4975044/4975277-80
Fax: 4975295

IDBI Bank Ltd.
Chaturvedi Mansion, 2nd Floor,
26/4, Old Palasia,
Agra Mumbai Road,
Indore 452 001.
Tel/Fax: 556666

Corporate Office:
Nariman Bhavan, 12th Floor,
Vinay K. Shah Marg,
Nariman Point,
Mumbai 400 021.
Tel: 2844473
Fax: 2844465

Indusind Bank Ltd.
IndusInd House,
425 Dadasaheb Bhadkamkar Marg,
Mumbai 400 004.
Tel: 3857474
Fax: 3859931
Email:
SUHAS.INDusbk@axcess net.IN

Times Bank Ltd.
Times of India Building
Dr. D.N. Road, Mumbai 400 001.
Tel: 2679951-55
Fax: 2679944/49

UTI Bank Ltd.
13th Floor, MakerTowers 'F',
Cuffe Parade, Colaba,
Mumbai 400 005.
Tel: 2189106107/08
Fax: 218694412181429
Email: co.ed@UTIBank.sprintrpg.
EMS.VSNL.net.in

APPENDIX C

References

Bhargava, U.K. *FERA 1973*. New Delhi: Taxmann Publications, 1995.

Brealey, Nicholas. *Asia Rising*. London: Michael Bloomberg, 1996.

Burns, J.F. *India Now Winning U.S. Investment*. USA: The New York Times, 1995.

Chokshi C.C. and Co *Budget 1997*. Bombay: Touche Ross & Co, 1997.

Department of Economics and Statistics, Government of India. *Statistical Outline of India, 1996–97*. Bombay: Tata Donnelley Limited, 1996.

Government of India, Ministry of Finance, Economic Division. *Economic Survey 1995–96: an update*. New Delhi: Government of India Press, 1996.

Indira Gandhi Institute of Development Research. *India Development Report*. New Delhi: Oxford University Press,1997.

Jain, Nabhi Kumar. *Income Tax Ready Reckoner*. New Delhi: Nabhi Publications, 1997.

Jain, R.K. *Central Excise Tariff 1997–98*. New Delhi: Centax Publications, 1997.

Jain, Rajiv. *Guide on Foreign Collaborations—Legal Parameters*. New Delhi: India Investment Publication, 1996.

_____. *Guide on Foreign Collaboration Policies and Procedures*. New Delhi: India Investment Publication, 1996.

Kumar, Nagesh. *Evaluation of Direct Foreign Investment in India*. New Delhi: Delhi Universtiy, 1980.

Ministry of Information & Broadcasting. *India 1995*. New Delhi: Gowarsons Publications,1995.

Nasierowski, W. "Doing Business in India". *Business Quarterly*. USA: 1991.

Patel, G.S. *Stock Exchanges in India*. A.D. Bombay: Shroff Memorial Trust, 1987.

Salamat Ali. *All Asia Guide* (15th edition compendium). Hong Kong: Review Publishing Co., 1996.

Seshan, P.A., et al. *Survey of Indian Industry 1995*. Madras: Kasturi & Sons Ltd.,1995.

Seth, Dilip. *Treatise on FERA*. New Delhi: Bharat Publishing House, 1993.

Varadarajan, P.R. *Journal of Business Research*. New York: Elsevier Science Inc., 1994.

About the Author

Born in India, HIRU BIJLANI holds a doctorate in business policy and administration from the University of Bombay. He has undergone advanced management training in various institutes and conducts seminars in India and abroad. A management consultant for over 14 years, he is currently president of the Institute of Management Consultants of India. He has managerial experience in diverse organisations in India, Africa and the Gulf and has been a director in several of them. He has written numerous articles, and his published books include *Globalisation—an overview*, *A Guide to Global Joint Ventures and Alliances* and *Tips and Tales for Travellers* (Times Editions).

Index